Love Thy

"Far too little has been written about what it means to be a Christian colleague in the workplace. Since that is where most Christians spend much of their lives, the omission is a glaring one. In this book, Will Morris fills the gap admirably. He observes the workplace with an astute pastoral eye, devotes each chapter to a different type of colleague and works out Christian responses in terms of the Parable of the Good Samaritan. Imaginatively conceived and engagingly written, *Love Thy Colleague* is at once confidently and openly Christian. Those hungry to know how to follow Jesus from 'nine to five' will be nourished; those who don't yet follow, will be drawn."

Nigel Biggar, Regius Professor of Moral and Pastoral Theology, and Director of the McDonald Centre for Theology, Ethics, and Public Life, at the University of Oxford

"Few people are better qualified to write about being authentically Christian at work than William Morris, a priest at St Martin-in-the-Fields and a Director of Global Tax Policy. Grounding himself in Jesus' endlessly fascinating parable of the Good Samaritan, Morris takes the reader through a tour of the weird and wonderful people who we found ourselves working alongside and poses the challenging question: what would happen if we viewed our colleagues like neighbour in Jesus' parable? The result is a book that is insightful, witty and wise."

Nick Spencer, Theos

"For too long the Church has paid only lip service to the world of work and yet this is where the majority of adults spend their waking hours. The challenge of working with an overbearing manager or a tedious colleague, or seeking to maintain one's personal integrity in the face of decidedly grey business practices pass many clergy by, but not William Morris. As an Anglican priest and an international tax-lawyer, he inhabits this world on a daily basis. As a result he brings to his writing not only a wisdom honed in the workplace, but one infused with spirituality and the insights of faith."

The Right Reverend Robert Atwell, Bishop of Exeter

Robert - with thanks
for your friendship
and
inspiration
William

LOVE thy colleague

Being authentically Christian at work

WILLIAM MORRIS

MONARCH
BOOKS

Oxford UK, and Grand Rapids, USA

Published by Monarch Books
an imprint of
Lion Hudson IP Ltd
Wilkinson House, Jordan Hill Road,
Oxford OX2 8DR, England
Email: monarch@lionhudson.com
www.lionhudson.com/monarch

ISBN 978 0 85721 716 5
e-ISBN 978 0 85721 717 2

First edition 2017

Acknowledgments
Cover images © Varijanta/iStockphoto

Scripture quotations marked NRSV are from The New Revised Standard Version of the Bible copyright © 1989 by the Division of Christian Education of the National Council of Churches in the USA. Used by permission. All Rights Reserved.

Scripture quotations marked NIV taken from the Holy Bible, New International Version Anglicised. Copyright © 1979, 1984, 2011 Biblica, formerly International Bible Society. Used by permission of Hodder & Stoughton Ltd, an Hachette UK company. All rights reserved. "NIV" is a registered trademark of Biblica. UK trademark number 1448790.

A catalogue record for this book is available from the British Library

Printed and bound in Great Britain by Marston Book Services Ltd, Oxfordshire

To my father

Derek Hazlitt Morris

1931–2016

With thanks for a lifetime of inspiration

and with much love

CONTENTS

ACKNOWLEDGMENTS

I owe thanks to two sets of people: those without whom this book would not have happened; and those who have helped me to make it better.

In the first category are my friends at Lion Hudson, particularly Tony Collins and Simon Cox. Tony took my second book forward for approval, even before the first had been published. And Simon, as his successor, had to endure my request for numerous extensions, as well as shepherding through the process two fairly dramatic reshapings of the structure of the book. All this he did with good humour and touching faith that a serviceable manuscript would emerge! I owe Simon and Tony a huge debt of gratitude.

In the category of those who have helped make this book better, two priests deserve special mention: my vicar at St Martin-in-the-Fields, Sam Wells; and my spiritual director of the past eight years, Robert Wiggs. The inspiration from Sam as a brilliant writer and preacher would merit a mention on its own – but he has done much more besides for this book. In addition to reading and commenting on several of the chapters, he also helped me shape the original book proposal and the two revisions. When I was ready to give up in the summer of 2016 and return the book advance, he persuaded me to stick with it a little longer and have another go – which I did. But his most important and most direct impact on the book was to suggest the twist on the parable of the Good

Samaritan. He encouraged me to imagine not just the ways we would offer mercy as the Good Samaritan, but also what might happen if we were the injured man lying in the road. That was a real gift, not least because it made me look much harder at myself, and at my own weaknesses. And Robert has also played a crucial role, reading most of the chapters (some more than once) and introducing me to writers such as Josef Pieper. He also constantly (and beneficially) questioned my sunny, Pollyannaish, potentially Pelagian view of the world, often triggering major rewrites. And all this he has done with enormous enthusiasm and encouragement for the project. He is already wondering what the third book will be about...

I owe thanks to my GE colleagues, Pat Brown and Marlin Risinger, who (even while the latter despaired of my singular usage of plural pronouns) offered helpful comments and picked up numerous typos. And thanks also to Chris Flowers, faithful Episcopalian/Anglican, who read and commented on a number of the chapters.

I also owe a debt of thanks to my other clergy colleagues at St Martin's – Richard, Katherine, Jonathan, and Alastair, in particular – who enabled me, just about, to keep the show on the road by picking up services as I regularly dropped them, and who have, even more importantly, been so encouraging of this project in clergy meetings, and elsewhere, as it has slowly inched along. Among the congregation, Leena Baxter has also offered constant encouragement.

And, finally, to return to the first category, my family deserve a huge amount of thanks. My father, the dedicatee of the book, died last summer while I was still becalmed, but every time we spoke he wanted to know how it was going – and he remains my model for a Christian at work. My mother has continued in her slightly bemused support – very proud, even if it's not quite her cup of tea! This book has not impinged as much as the first one did on the lives of Alex, Julia, and Kat, but they have, nevertheless, been most tolerant when it did. And Michelle – who did have to watch me spend much of our last summer holiday at work on this, as well as on countless occasions since – has again shouldered the load of keeping the Morris family moving forward in good order, even as she wonders whether me doing two or three jobs at the same time really is that sensible...

INTRODUCTION

From time to time I get invited to talk to faith-based groups about God and work. I'm aware that for many of the people I'm talking to, those are two words that simply don't go together. Faith and worship; faith and prayer; faith and compassion; faith and social action; faith and family – yes, all those go together. But faith and work? Especially faith and for-profit work? There's something wrong there.

I could launch into a theological explanation of why they do go together. But, in fact, however sophisticated the group, I always find it better to start with the Bible. Whether we believe it literally, metaphorically, poetically, or some other way, the Bible speaks vividly to our faith in a God who created the world, who loves us deeply, and who in the end will make all things perfect – however hard we have tried to ensure in the interim that doesn't happen.

So, I start with the (first) creation story in Genesis 1 – the story of a worker God who pauses at the end of each day to see what He has created, what He has made, and thinks that it is good. A God who delights in creating, in making things, in working. And a God who spends the whole week at work, making the world – the whole world. Not just churches or holy places; and not just on Sunday mornings. One Creator God, one created world, one completely integrated week.

Then I go right to the other end of the Bible and read them the end of the book of Revelation. About the new heaven and the new earth; the new Jerusalem descending out of heaven, and God saying "See, I am making all things new." This is God again as creator, working and remaking things. And making everything new, the whole of the created world, every aspect of it: not just the Temple, and not just the Sabbath.

I then ask a slightly rhetorical question. "Why is it," I wonder, "that God is so interested in everything, as a worker, at the beginning of the world, and is so interested in everything, as a worker, at the end of the world, yet in the middle of that time – the present – is completely disinterested in work, and only cares about church and Sundays? Why," I go on, "is He so generous at the beginning and at the end, and yet in the middle where we – His creation, made in His image – live and work, is He so much less generous, so much less concerned about His creation, so much less interested in anything other than church-based worship? Does that really make sense?" I ask them. "Why doesn't He also care just as much right now about the whole of His creation, including the world of work?"

Well, I believe, of course, that He does. I believe that God really cares about the world of work. Some still object, however, that God as the creator – both at the beginning and at the end – is totally different from us as workers in the middle of time, the here-and-now. So, prepared for that question, I take them back to Genesis, this time to chapter 2. In Genesis 2, in the second creation story, God creates humankind to be workers with Him: "The Lord God took the man[1] and put him in the garden of Eden to till it and keep it" (2:15 NRSV). So, we were created by God to help work and care for His creation.

But, the sceptics will say, that was in the perfection of the garden of Eden, at the beginning. What about now, with bad bosses; difficult colleagues; ridiculous, petty rules; the spread

---

1   This truly means all humankind, not just men. In the narrative of Genesis, however, woman has not yet been created – just one of a number of differences between the first and second creation stories in Genesis 1 and 2.

of zero-hours contracts; pressure to work long hours; the threat of redundancy; and so on? How can God be interested in this? How can there be anything of Him in that?

So, then I take them on one further chapter in the narrative, to Genesis 3. It would, of course, be completely foolish to argue that every workplace is perfect, and that every job is fulfilling, but the root of that problem lies in us humans, not with God. The expulsion from the garden of Eden spells out that truth when God tells Adam that because he did what he was told not to do, "cursed is the ground because of you; in toil you shall eat of it all the days of your life; thorns and thistles it shall bring forth for you; and you shall eat the plants of the field. By the sweat of your face you shall eat bread until you return to the ground" (3:17–19 NRSV). Long story short: we messed up, but we still have to work; and because of who we now are, that work will not always be easy.

But that's not the end of the story, even though it helps to explain where we currently find ourselves. The interest of God at the beginning and the end of time, the narrative story of the people of Israel in the Old Testament, and the salvation offered by Christ in the New Testament, all point to the fact that what God really wants for the world, and for humanity, is its redemption, its healing – including the world of work. Even if we've messed it up, God wants us to help realize more of its potential. Perfection will not come again until the end of time, but we, as God's children – His co-workers, His hands and feet on earth working with the Holy Spirit – do have the chance to make a little better the things that we've so badly messed up, including in our workplace. And we can do that right here, right now, today.

So how do we go about that? Well, of course, as individuals, the workplace is somewhere we can exercise personal responsibility and behave ethically. Where we can earn the money that feeds and clothes our family. Where we get the satisfaction of doing an honest day's work for an honest day's pay. But there are many opportunities beyond that. You'll be surprised at just how many ways there are in the workplace to help others – our neighbours at work; how many ways there are to show God's love to our colleagues. Whether it's an office, a factory, a shop, or a school:

- It can be a place where we fulfil our obligation as Christians to care for those who are in need – our neighbours; those in our workplace who (to adapt slightly the parable of the sheep and the goats) are metaphorically hungry, or thirsty, or are always the stranger, or feel naked, or consider themselves a prisoner.

- It can be a place where we exercise the gifts and talents that God has given us, in making things and providing services that people need. In doing that, we are also creating employment for others that gives them dignity and enables them to support their families, as well as creating wealth that can then be shared with others.

- It can be a place where we are co-workers in the healing of God's creation, which has been fractured because of our imperfections, by working for fairness and ethics in our own business and by encouraging that business to contribute more generally to the common good of the community and society around it.

- It can be a place where we bring our experience of Jesus to those who may not know Him – perhaps not by overtly preaching the good news, but more by the example of the way we lead our lives, and the way we treat others, while being open about our Christian belief and motivation.

To return, then, to my earlier question – why would God not be interested in the workplace, when all that opportunity exists there? Well, my answer, of course, is that He is! So I hope that you will find support and encouragement here as you seek, with God, to improve your workplace and as you seek to help your colleagues. I hope you'll find what richness there is in being the neighbour to those colleagues – and what richness there is in loving your colleague as yourself.

Will Morris
London, May 2017

1

WHO IS MY NEIGHBOUR AT WORK?

Just then a lawyer stood up to test Jesus. "Teacher," he said, "what must I do to inherit eternal life?" He said to him, "What is written in the law? What do you read there?" He answered, "You shall love the Lord your God with all your heart, and with all your soul, and with all your strength, and with all your mind; and your neighbour as yourself." And he said to him, "You have given the right answer; do this, and you will live."

But wanting to justify himself, he asked Jesus, "And who is my neighbour?" Jesus replied, "A man was going down from Jerusalem to Jericho, and fell into the hands of robbers, who stripped him, beat him, and went away, leaving him half dead. Now by chance a priest was going down that road; and when he saw him, he passed by on the other side. So likewise a Levite, when he came to the place and saw him, passed by on the other side. But

a Samaritan while travelling came near him;
and when he saw him, he was moved with pity.
He went to him and bandaged his wounds,
having poured oil and wine on them. Then he
put him on his own animal, brought him to an
inn, and took care of him. The next day he took
out two denarii, gave them to the innkeeper,
and said, 'Take care of him; and when I come
back, I will repay you whatever more you
spend.' Which of these three, do you think,
was a neighbour to the man who fell into the
hands of the robbers?" He said, "The one who
showed him mercy." Jesus said to him, "Go
and do likewise."

Luke 10:25–37 NRSV

Right out of school, my first job was working in a French
bank at the minimum wage doing whatever relatively
unskilled tasks needed doing. After a short while my
employers decided I was just the right guy to mark each of the
hundreds of cheques that our customers deposited each day
with a magnetic number in the bottom right hand corner. It
may not sound terribly exciting, but it was, truly, one of the
formative experiences of my life. However, when I started I did
face three small problems: first, I had absolutely no idea what I
was doing; second, despite my assertions to the contrary when
I was interviewed, I actually spoke no French; and third, I had
no friends (or even acquaintances) in Bordeaux.

But as the months passed three rather wonderful things
happened: some of my colleagues took pity on me and showed
me how to do the job; others of them helped me with my
French; and a third set of colleagues, although often much
older than I and from completely different backgrounds,

invited me round for dinner, or out to a movie, or to go to the beach. That workplace was certainly not perfect, and by no means was everyone happy, but, because of that kindness shown to me as I initially struggled, it remains one of the most fulfilling of all my work experiences.

Neighbour... neighbourliness... neighbourhood

We tend to view the workplace through a dystopian lens, whether it's that of a Dilbert cartoon, or a TV show like *The Office*, or a movie like *Wall Street*. But it doesn't have to be like that. It doesn't have to be a place of alienation; a place of purely transactional interactions; a place of only sterile, antiseptic relationships. It can be so much more – and yet it so often isn't. Why does it seem so hard, given the story I've just told? Well, you might say, your story could only have happened to an unthreatening teenager in a relatively low-pressured environment. What if I had been an ambitious permanent employee in a cut-throat business in my twenties; or a harassed, irascible, over-stretched new parent trying to find a work–life balance in my thirties; or a lazy, gossipy, middle-aged freeloader drifting through my forties; or an incompetent, out-of-touch, just-hanging-on-for-my-pension boss in my fifties? Would my colleagues have been so kind then? Would they have cared? It's a fair question. Some colleagues in the workplace can be incredibly difficult to approach, far less like. And when we are always being pushed to go harder and faster, when we constantly have to worry about our jobs, it's tough to find the time to think about others. It is emotionally so much easier to keep our distance; so much more unambiguous (and fun, sometimes) to be judgmental; so much less effort if we restrict our involvement to the bare minimum. Of course, we'd rarely put it that way… but if we narrow our scope so that care is something only to be doled out when we have the time, is something only to be awarded based on whether the person is deserving or not, then the workplace loses much of its potential to be transformational in our lives – loses that potential that I experienced all those years ago.

So how do we foster work relationships, and an atmosphere in the workplace, that together can move us beyond those rather narrow, purely transactional interactions into which we can all-too-easily slip? And how do we do it in a way that enables us to have those relationships with difficult people as well as easy people; with unsympathetic people as well as engaging ones; with older people as well as younger ones; with more senior colleagues as well as junior ones? Well, I think – I hope – the answer may lie in a single word, although a big one: "neighbour". If we can view all of our colleagues as our neighbours, our entire workplace as a neighbourhood, and our obligation (and privilege) to all of our fellow workers as neighbourliness, then perhaps we can start to build relationships that don't rely on how much we like our colleague, or how deserving they are. And if we can do that, then we will also begin to see our work as a place that God cares about, as a place where He Himself is at work, and as a place where we can work with Him.

Who is my neighbour?

But, as I said, neighbour is a big word that needs unpacking. Who is our "neighbour", and what does it mean to be a "neighbour"? To answer that I want to explore one of the best known of all Jesus' parables – the parable of the Good Samaritan. We may think we know the story well: someone gets hurt; another person helps him; and we'd do the same. But there's actually much more to it than that, and if we dig into the story we'll unearth the complexity, and potential richness, of what it can mean to be a neighbour at work.

The parable asks four questions: two explicit ones, and two implicit ones. And, I believe, it is only in answering all four that we can fully understand the idea of neighbourliness, of being a neighbour at work.

- The first (explicit) question in the parable is this: who is my neighbour?

- The second (implicit) question is: am I the Good Samaritan – or another character in the story?

- The third (explicit) question is: who was the neighbour to this man?

- The fourth (implicit) question is: what does it mean to be the Good Samaritan?

We'll look at each question in turn, and, in doing that, hopefully we can begin to answer the central question of this book, which my French colleagues seemed to understand so effortlessly (if implicitly) all those years ago: how do we truly love our neighbour at work? How do we truly love our colleague?

Offering mercy: who is my neighbour?

The first question asked in the parable seems straightforward: who is my neighbour? The lawyer who asks it has just – correctly – told Jesus that one of the things he must do to inherit eternal life is to love his neighbour as himself. But then, seeking to justify himself, he overreaches. It's not unreasonable to suspect that he thought that he already knew the answer and was looking for further validation from Jesus. For him it may have seemed a simple question. Who was his neighbour?

It was the person who lived in his (nice) neighbourhood; his fellow (well-educated) lawyers; those who worshipped in the same (sophisticated) way as him; his fellow Jews (as long as they were of a certain standing). We are tribal animals, and the lawyer may well have seen it in those terms. His neighbours were the deserving members of his tribe. And perhaps, as I've noted above, we would see it the same at work today. Our neighbours are the likeable people in the workspace around us; the deserving members of our team; the good people in our department. But Jesus was having none of that. So, to answer the question about who the lawyer's neighbour is, He tells the lawyer a story about someone who could never have been in his tribe.

But the story that Jesus tells also has an unusual twist, because it requires the lawyer (and us) to imagine himself in it. And it is in this effort of imagining that Jesus asks the lawyer (and us) the parable's second question: which character am I in the parable? Now, while it may not be true for everyone, I think many of us (me, certainly) almost automatically see ourselves as the Good Samaritan – whether at home, at church, or in the workplace; as the socially aware, generous, thoughtful giver who cares for the neighbour in need. But we need to be a little careful, because Jesus is not here to validate our own self-image. There are other characters in addition to the Good Samaritan that are available to be played by us – the priest and Levite, for example. So, we need to ask ourselves whether we can be absolutely certain that we are not (unpleasant though the thought is) one of the characters who passes by on the other side. Or, perhaps, might we be the lawyer who asks the (self-justificatory) question: who is my neighbour? Are we really always the Good Samaritan, the good neighbour?

To explore – against what we might think are our own broad, generous views on whom we would view as our "neighbour", as well as which character in the parable we might be – I want, based on my own experience, to reimagine the parable a couple of different ways in a modern workplace setting, in my own "neighbourhood". As will quickly become clear, I don't always come out as well as my French colleagues did…

- There was someone in another department who, I heard third-hand, had a child who was seriously ill. Now, of course, if this had been someone closer to me, whom I knew well, I wouldn't have hesitated to try to comfort them. But this other person? Well, I wondered, might it not be a bit intrusive or even a little presumptuous for me to offer them comfort when I hardly knew them? Perhaps it might even do more harm than good? Perhaps, I eventually told myself, they were just a little too far from me for me to be a real neighbour.

- There was a person who was forever gossiping. It wasn't particularly nasty or scurrilous gossip, but, like a low-grade fever, it never seemed to go away and it ever so slightly soured the workplace atmosphere. Then one day I heard a truly scurrilous piece of gossip about them. Really bad. And they knew lots of people knew about it. More particularly, they knew that I knew. And I could see them shrinking back as I came towards them. But I felt a natural ambivalence – after all, those who live by the sword die by it, don't they? They really are just not quite as deserving. And anyway, when it came right down to it, I reassured myself, even though it was really bad gossip, it was only words, and those (unlike sticks and stones) wouldn't really hurt them – at least after a while.

- I had a colleague who was having difficulty with their job. But I was pretty stretched, too. If I had had a little more time I would have really loved to help out. But I didn't have time, and anyway I had to think about my own job at what was a tricky time for the company. Besides which, I told myself, training someone to do their job more efficiently was really my boss's job (or HR's, or someone else's), so, much as I'd really have liked to help (really), I had to prioritize.

- A colleague who had a reputation for being a fairly generous spender came to me and explained that they really needed to borrow some money for a month or so. I could tell it had been incredibly difficult – and deeply embarrassing – for them to ask me for a loan, but I couldn't quite get over their breach of a sacred taboo in asking me for money. So, I rationalized that I might need the money, and I might never get paid back, and, anyway, why couldn't my colleague go to their own bank, or borrow from their own family?

- I had a colleague accused of a serious ethics violation. I'd known the person a long time and couldn't quite believe it was true. I really wanted to speak up for them, but I just wasn't sure. So, I told myself that I had to think about my own job. And what if the allegation were true? I couldn't afford to be tainted with that same brush, because my family was depending on me. And besides, our internal disciplinary process was very fair, I rationalized, so this was not going to be a lynching by management. Anyway, perhaps there really was no smoke without fire.

Offering mercy: am I the Good Samaritan?

Now, perhaps you would have stopped and tended the injured person in some or all of those cases. But I know that I, in each case – and however much I might like to think myself the Good Samaritan – passed by on the other side. Because these were the special cases, I would tell myself. Because the person wasn't quite a member of my tribe; or wasn't entirely deserving;

or I didn't really have the time; or I didn't feel completely comfortable lending money to someone unreliable for what was, quite possibly, a dubious cause; or I had to look out for my own job. But, completely natural, totally understandable though each of these rationalizations is in human terms, I don't think Jesus would have given them much time. So, let's run through each of them in turn, and the implications each has for the meaning of the word "neighbour".

First, there's the question of whether I need to know someone well for them to be my neighbour. While we are not explicitly told, I think we can assume that the Good Samaritan did not know the injured man. In the parable, personal acquaintance with, or common belonging to, a group or tribe is not a necessary qualification for being a neighbour. Second, does my neighbour need to be deserving of my help? Well, again, the Good Samaritan knows nothing about the injured man, other than that he has been attacked and needs help. He doesn't know whether he's good or bad; deserving or undeserving; saint or sinner. He only knows that the injured man is in need, and that's enough. Third, there's the issue of whether I really don't have enough time to help. It seems that the Good Samaritan is a businessman. He may have been in just as much of a hurry (whether to get to the next deal, or to get back to his family) as the priest and the Levite were to get wherever they were going. But he makes the time, even though he, too, didn't have it – because someone needed him. Fourth, what about me feeling that I don't have quite enough money or other material resources to be able to help? Again, the Good Samaritan spends money, uses his own resources, on a man he doesn't know but who needs these resources. We don't know whether the Good Samaritan is rich or poor, just that he has enough to be able to say to the innkeeper (whom he also doesn't know, and has no reason to trust), "Do whatever it takes." And finally, what about what others might think of me? Well, despite what Jews said, thought about, and occasionally did to the Samaritans, this Samaritan doesn't care. Nor, for that matter does he care what his fellow Samaritans might think of him for helping out the injured man, whom we assume is a Jew.

While I condemn only myself in these reimaginings, perhaps these scenarios resonate with your experience in the workplace. It's not that I consciously, selfishly, refuse to help someone in need. It's more that in the murkiness and complexity and pressure of daily life, I'll seek the easier route, staying in my comfort zone, and passing by on the other side. We'll look at that in later chapters, but the important thing to note here is that while we always need to ask ourselves which character in the story we are, we shouldn't be completely depressed if we exhibit priestly or Levitical qualities. Jesus comes not to condemn us but to save us. So, this parable is not told to make us feel bad, but rather to make us answer the questions that Jesus asks us – and, through answering them, to challenge us, to change our perception of our comfort zone, to guide us to an understanding of what it means to be a neighbour: to love our colleague.

Offering mercy: to whom am I the neighbour?

Jesus also guides us in a different direction through the third question asked by the parable – this one posed explicitly by Jesus to the lawyer. And He achieves this change in direction by subverting the first explicit question. The lawyer – in order to justify himself further – asks Jesus: "Who is my neighbour?" But Jesus turns the question around in the parable. Instead of helping to define and delineate who was the neighbour of the priest or the Levite (or, for that matter, who was the neighbour of the Good Samaritan), rather He asks the lawyer another question: who was the neighbour to the injured man?

What's the difference there, you ask? Well, actually quite an important one. The lawyer's question assumes that "neighbour" is a defined group, almost a club, of people around us to whom we relate. We're at the centre; the others cluster around us. As we've already discussed, perhaps for the lawyer it was the people of Israel; or perhaps a more select group associated with the Temple; or perhaps those who belonged to a certain sect; or those who followed certain purification rites. Whichever it was, "neighbour" for the lawyer was an identifiable attribute of other people. But Jesus, by turning the question around, undercuts all that. Suddenly "neighbour" is not someone else – it's you. No longer is it another person who is the neighbour to us; it is we who are the neighbour to others. "Neighbour" is no longer defined by other people's characteristics, or upbringing, or accident of birth; it's defined by our reaction to another person (as happened to me in France). To his credit – hope for us all! – the lawyer sees what Jesus has done. He doesn't prevaricate, or hesitate: the neighbour, he says, is the one who showed mercy to the injured man. The neighbour is the person who realized that the injured man was in need, and without any thought as to whether the man was in the right club, followed the right rules, or ate the right food, helped him – showed him mercy. "Go and do likewise," Jesus tells him; "Go and do likewise," Jesus tells us.

This reversal of our understanding of neighbour leads us towards the answer to the fourth and last (implicit) question asked by the parable: what does it mean to be the Good Samaritan? My neighbour – the one I am supposed to love – is not defined by proximity to me (the tax team); or similarity to me (university or profession); or identity of interest with me (food, movies); or friendship with me. And it is especially not defined by whether someone is a fellow Christian. Not because any of these things are not important in day-today interactions, but because in this case, to look at those factors is to ask the wrong question; it is to look through the telescope the wrong way. "Neighbour" is not what someone else is to me; it is what I am to someone else. I and you are the neighbour, when someone – anyone – is in need, and we show "mercy",[2] compassion, caring. It was this that happened to me in France; others became a neighbour to me. And it is this understanding in the office, if I can recapture it, that offers that transformational potential. This is what it means to be the Good Samaritan to someone else.

Offering mercy: loving your neighbour and yourself

There is one other, vital, point to be made about being a neighbour to others. Everything we have looked at so far sounds a little austere, perhaps even a little high minded. It seems to be about all the things we have to do, and how we so often fail to do them. And it's true that the answer to that fourth, final question – what does it mean to be the Good Samaritan? – is undoubtedly to offer mercy to those who need it. But there's really quite a lot more to the answer than just that.

Part of the good news in the parable is that, in fact, it's not just the injured man who benefits from the actions of the Good Samaritan, but also the Good Samaritan himself. As the lawyer reminds us, the commandment is "to love your neighbour as yourself". Two parts: neighbour and self. In his unconditional generosity, the Good Samaritan also benefits from helping another in need in a way that the priest and Levite do not. So, while expanding the number of people to whom we feel moved to show compassion and mercy is certainly an important

---

2   I mean "mercy" in the broader sense of the word, shed of its connotations of "leniency" or "clemency" for doing something wrong. In the parable the word is akin to kindness, generosity, etc.

(and beneficial) result of the parable, Jesus' focus is at least as much on the benefit to us of becoming the neighbour to someone else. The act of showing mercy – freely, generously given, without thought of reward or return – releases us from a mentality of scarcity where we dole out limited benefits to a defined circle. Instead, we are welcomed into a mentality of abundance where we can show mercy to anyone who needs it. Put slightly differently, instead of constantly worrying about how to make do with too little, we can have fun and derive joy from giving to others what we have too much of. Being a neighbour to others, showing them mercy, allows us to love ourselves as well. It frees us, it opens us up, it transforms us. It allows us to love ourselves as much as we love our neighbour – and the mercy shown to the other becomes mercy also shown to ourselves.

Accepting mercy: am I the injured man?

In this final section I want to point to one other potential reversal of roles which, once understood, further enriches the concept of "neighbour". To do that let's return to the second question asked by the parable – which character am I in the parable? In the list of other characters at the beginning of the chapter, I purposely omitted the injured man himself. But I now want to turn to him, because, if we are the injured person, that flips everything on its head. Whether we are the Good Samaritan, priest, Levite, or the questioning lawyer, we are able to offer mercy. The only difference comes in whether or not we actually do so. But what if, instead, we are the injured man lying in the road? Then we don't face a choice as to whether to be generous or not. Instead we face a choice as to whether to accept mercy or not; whether to acknowledge and receive mercy, or to reject it. *What does he mean?* you're thinking. Of course, if we're lying injured in the road we'll be hoping that someone turns up and helps us. And my reply is that, yes, in a literal sense we would hope for that, but the parable operates on us, the reader, on several levels beyond the literal. And on those metaphorical levels the injured man, the man desperately in need of healing, in fact thinks that he is hale and hearty and fully in control. In those circumstances, if anyone had the temerity to suggest that he needed help, far less was in need of "mercy", he'd laugh in their face, or worse.

So, what – on a metaphorical level – might Jesus have meant by talking about a man who needed healing but refused to accept that he was injured? Well, in Jesus' own time one such "man" was in fact a group – the people of Israel. Beloved of God, yet stubborn and proud, Israel was seething under the Roman heel, compromised and traduced by its leaders. Israel badly needed healing, even if it didn't recognize it. But another set of people who don't yet accept their need for healing exists today. That's you and me, as we go about our daily lives – including in the workplace. Healing is being offered; the Good Samaritan is ready to bind up our wounds. At the same time, stubborn, proud, and blind as we individually are, we may not know (or we may actively deny) that we are in any way sick. We may not see the Good Samaritan – Jesus – standing next to us.

As we have already seen, in the narrative of our lives we are always at the centre. In our own story, we are usually in control, usually strong. And if we're not, then we make excuses. If things aren't going quite right now, well, it's because we had a stroke of bad luck; or we were badly treated; or the system is rigged. But there's nothing wrong with *us*. It's everything else – on the outside – that's wrong. No, says Jesus, think again. It is in our pride and in our stubbornness; in our delusions of self-sufficiency and our refusal to recognize the source of our gifts; in our self-absorption and in our arrogance, that we are blinded to our desperate need for healing. It is in all of those that we fail to see what is in front of our eyes: that, spiritually, we are lying bloodied and battered in the road. We need healing, and we need it badly. But to be healed, we also need to accept that we have been wounded, that we are injured – and that can be really hard. Without doing that, however, we simply can't move on.

So, while we must certainly offer mercy to all those who need it – to our neighbour, to our colleague – we must also be prepared to accept mercy, from whomever and wherever it comes. To be sure, if we mess up we might expect (or, at least, hope) to be shown mercy, to be given a helping hand. But what, we might ask, could we possibly have to learn about our own need for healing, for example, from our lazy colleague, or our arrogant colleague, or our incompetent colleague? Well, as we'll see in later chapters, perhaps something, perhaps even quite a lot – something that will be "mercy" to us; a "weakness" of our colleague that brings to light our own need for healing that we have never recognized. So, for example, as we pity, and try to offer mercy to our insensitive colleague, perhaps we are ourselves over-sensitive; as we offer mercy to the lazy colleague, perhaps we are ourselves too busy; as we dispense healing to the ambitious colleague, perhaps we don't stretch ourselves enough. We need mercy, too.

Offering and accepting mercy at work

As we go through the rest of the book, we will try to apply – across a range of types and circumstances – this rich, complex idea of loving our neighbour, our colleague, in the neighbourhood that is the workplace. For us to be that neighbour does not require us to have a close friendship with every colleague – but, in every case, we will now progress beyond a dry and superficial professional relationship.

Because of the different basis, the set of beliefs, upon which this new relationship is based, it will allow us to act consistently not just when it's easy, but also when it's hard; not just when our colleagues are likeable, but also when they're unpleasant. In this new pattern, we no longer ask what people are to us, and if they are our neighbours. We ask, instead, how we can be a neighbour to those colleagues, despite the fact that it may be difficult, or painful, or expensive.

To further enrich the idea of "neighbour", we'll also ask whether, in the situations we examine, we may be the one in need of mercy, and how our colleagues may be able to be neighbours to us. We'll look at why we may be resistant to that mercy, but why we so badly need to accept it from the Good Samaritan – from Jesus.

We will learn how to love our neighbour, our colleague – and how to love ourselves. And, in all of this we will learn, once again, how to love our God, and how much He loves us.

2

THE AMBITIOUS COLLEAGUE

Do you not know that in a race all the runners run, but only one gets the prize? Run in such a way as to get the prize. Everyone who competes in the games goes into strict training. They do it to get a crown that will not last; but we do it to get a crown that will last forever. Therefore I do not run like someone running aimlessly; I do not fight like a boxer beating the air. No, I strike a blow to my body and make it my slave so that after I have preached to others, I myself will not be disqualified for the prize.

1 Corinthians 9:24–27 NIV

We've all had at least one ambitious colleague, and we probably remember them without much fondness. Sharp-elbowed, calculating, and self-promoting. Ingratiating upwards, dismissive downwards, and plain hostile sideways to their peers (their competitors). Never to be seen when the dull, necessary work was required; but always to be seen when something had a whiff of glamour, or the sponsorship of someone-who-mattered. Playing the office equivalent of 3-D chess: forever planning out which project or job could advance them to the next step; always wondering about the best placed person to serve as an acolyte; always thinking, planning, scheming ahead. When I started my first job as a lawyer, the track to partnership was about eight years, our intake of trainee lawyers was over thirty, and the expectation was that perhaps five or so of us would make it (in fact, a couple of recessions later, it was only two). The equation was fairly straightforward: bad odds and high stakes = fierce competition.

Convinced, almost before I'd arrived (and certainly within a few weeks of being there), that I had not so much chosen the wrong firm to work at, as the completely wrong profession, I began planning my escape and counting the days. This gave me a ringside seat from which to observe the more ambitious of my colleagues. Volunteers to go to the printers all night to proof-read offer documents? Up went the usual hands. Weekend work? The usual suspects. Another (at least, at our junior level) mind-numbing mega-deal or privatization? Same again. And always circling around the partners, preventing the rest of us from getting close to those partners (had we wanted to…), laughing at their bad jokes, complimenting them extravagantly, and, of course, subtly denigrating the competition (us) if it appeared to offer even the slightest possibility of getting ahead. The cost of their ambition – at least it seemed to me – far outweighed any potential gain, and yet they pursued the prize persistently and relentlessly. On and on.

Ambition: with adjectives

"Ambition" is one of those words that seems to attract unattractive adjectives: blind, proud, single-minded, misplaced, arrogant, overweening, ruthless, selfish, deadly. In the workplace, it tends to be synonymous with personal advancement. We've all seen it, and not just in relation to young, junior staff (like me and my first colleagues) who have a valuable but elusive prize held in front of them – always slightly out of reach – but in relation to people at all levels. The CEO who launches the (disruptive) takeover to make their name as a titan of industry. The CFO who boosts short-term profit to be a hero with the market and lift the share price (and their stock options). The HR manager who designs a new internal assessment system (that unsettles everyone) to demonstrate their leadership. The company bean-counter, seeking to stand out as the champion of the bottom line, who finds new ways to shave spending that result in tangible savings, but very real intangible (often human) costs. The health and safety officer who devises yet another approval process that ties people up in knots before something/anything can be done, to enhance their reputation as a safe pair of hands. Ambition can be not only unpleasant, but also costly.

And this is not new, not just a phenomenon of the twenty-first century, or of capitalism, but something deep in the human psyche. The Bible has plenty of highly critical things to say about ambition, too. In the story of Jesus' time in the wilderness in Matthew's Gospel, the devil tries to tempt Jesus by taking Him to a high mountain and showing Him "all the kingdoms of the world and their splendour", laid out before Him. "All these I will give you, if you will fall down and worship me," the devil says. But Jesus curtly rejects him (Matthew 4:8–10 NRSV). In another passage, later in Matthew, Jesus talks at length about the scribes and Pharisees whose ambition is to be thought well of for their wisdom and their piety; to be accorded the place of honour at the table and in the synagogue; and to be recognized for their generosity. "Truly, I tell you," Jesus tells the crowd, "they have received their reward" (Matthew 6:2 NRSV). And, to give one more example, Paul, in his letter to the Philippians, says: "Do nothing from selfish ambition or conceit, but in humility regard others as better than yourselves" (Philippians 2:3 NRSV). Case closed: ambition is bad. Always has been. And our ambitious colleague is, therefore, at best, misguided; at worst, proud, arrogant, blind, etc.

Perhaps, we should pause for a second, not least because that last sentence is interesting. The previously unattractive adjectives that qualified "ambition" have become standalone (although still unattractive) characteristics. Put a little more simply, perhaps "ambition" is the name under which we loosely group a number of fundamental human traits that we don't terribly like (or, at least, feel ashamed of). So, isn't it possible that the problem isn't "ambition", as such, but is pride, or arrogance, or blindness, and what those attributes make us do? If that is the case, then what might "ambition" be? What does it mean, relieved of those unappealing characteristics?

Ambition: wanting to do something

At its most basic, ambition is a desire to do something, as opposed to a desire to do nothing, although not literally, of course, in the work context. When most of us go to work, we do "something", engage in some activity, because even if we dislike our jobs we understand that we have to give some labour in return for the reward that we get. What I mean, rather, is that ambition is linked to a desire to change, to alter, and, perhaps, to grow something. This can be done in bad, damaging ways (proudly, arrogantly, blindly, etc.), but might it also have a positive aspect, even some godly potential? To explore that further, it might be helpful to look at the opposite of my definition of ambition – movement, action, growth. The early monks believed in a state they called "acedia" (or accidie, or accedie). It was thought by the Desert Fathers and others to be the forerunner of "sloth" or laziness (which we'll look at in another chapter). It refers to a state of lassitude, or lethargy; or, again, put slightly differently, to an inability to motivate ourselves, or get going. It was viewed as a serious problem because it made a person not simply inactive, but caused them to withdraw and disengage from the world. We are put on this earth, the monks thought, to be in relationship with God's people, with God's earth, and with God Himself. If we withdraw from those, then we are rejecting our reason for being.

Put in that way – ambition vs acedia; something vs nothing – perhaps there might be an upside to ambition? To help explore that, let's turn to the passage at the start of this chapter from Paul's first letter to the Corinthians. The quarrelsome Christians of Corinth arguably had too much ambition of the proud, arrogant, blind variety. But although Paul does spend much time telling them to grow up ("I could not speak to you as spiritual people, but rather as people of the flesh, as infants in Christ. I fed you with milk, not solid food, for you were not ready for solid food. Even now you are still not ready…" (3:1–2 NRSV)), Paul does not tell them simply to be gentle and kind, and to rein in their ambition. Rather, he purposely uses two highly competitive sporting analogies to steer the Corinthians in a more positive direction. "Just as the runner who wants to win the race trains and runs hard because there can only be one winner," he tells the Corinthians, "so, too, must you train hard. And you must focus – focus – not run aimlessly." Likewise, switching to a boxing analogy, he tells them: "When I box, I don't do air punches. I punch to win, and so should you."

Paul's metaphors indicate that a desire – the ambition – to achieve something important, to "win a crown", is acceptable, but that the way in which we do it is also important. Not proudly, arrogantly, blindly, to be sure, but with strict training, determination, and a will to win. So, in light of that, let's revisit some of the examples of ambition I mentioned at the beginning of the chapter, and see whether "ambition" could lead to a positive outcome.

- The CEO and the takeover. The disruptive vanity project has nothing to recommend it. But a takeover or merger that results in genuine synergies (i.e. more than simply job losses), that results in a stronger overall group, that results in a better, more productive, more secure future for the acquired company – that will be a net positive. To be sure, it may be disruptive, some relaxed working practices may get changed and some comfort zones invaded, but there may also be something genuinely creative in that combination.

- The CFO and the numbers. Likewise, a CFO who massages the quarterly numbers to win the acclaim of the market is not a hero. But a CFO who perceives that value is being locked up in the company and that the stock price is truly undervalued may be justified in trying to get the price up. Why? Because a higher stock price may enable the company to raise more capital, to invest that capital, and, thereby, to increase productivity. And while a higher stock price may help the CFO's stock options, there are lots of other stakeholders in businesses who also benefit: especially those receiving modest pensions from pension funds that invest in the company's stock.

- The new HR process. An HR manager who invents yet another complex system for measuring and advancing employee careers may simply be seeking to reinvent the wheel to benefit themselves. But, at the same time, there is little that is more important inside many companies than the "human capital" that drives the business; so, treating people well, and managing their careers so that both they and the company get the best outcome are truly important. An improvement in an imperfect process can really help people.

- The cost-cutter. Then there is the ambitious internal accountant who sees only numbers rather than people, and who cuts the latter as though they were the former, to meet numerically possible – but humanely impossible – targets. That person only subtracts; never adds. But inside a business large or small, the fact remains that employees are generally spending someone else's money, and must, therefore, account for that. Furthermore, spending tends to go on auto-pilot; once started, it rarely stops of its own accord, never shrinks, and often grows. But the fact that spending might have been necessary and justified at one time does not mean that it will always continue to be, and does not mean it is not worth reconsidering that from time to time. Funds are not limitless, and unnecessary spending may be preventing more productive spending in another area.

- A better, safer workplace. Finally, health and safety has gained a bad, risk-averse, "jobsworth"[3] reputation. Another paradise for ambitious but petty minds. But when you look back even a couple of decades at the lax attitude to industrial injuries, exposure to toxic materials in the workplace, and even office-based injuries such as RSIs and all the problems attendant on sitting at a desk for eight hours a day, health and safety doesn't look quite so foolish. Again, changes which make the workplace a safer, but also more productive and enjoyable place, can be real benefits.

---

3   For the non-British reader, this derives from the common bureaucratic excuse: "It's more than my job's worth" not to enforce this, that, or the other petty rule.

There are many dangers for us in ambition, both collectively and individually. But there are also dangers for us in the lack of it, for from that, nothing will come. There is nothing of real life in listlessness and torpor; in being stuck in a rut; in doing today what you know you will also do tomorrow simply because it's what you did yesterday. That is the acedia that makes us slowly withdraw from the world, disengage from the work which is where we can love our colleagues, and pull back from our fellow humans with whom we are called to be in relationship, to whom we are called upon to show mercy.

To close out this point, acedia may well sound theoretical and remote, but I remember a colleague who, several years ago, embodied both the problem and the solution. This colleague had a mid-ranked job, but was marked out for bigger things. The problem was that they had grown too comfortable in their job. They did it well, but it no longer challenged them. Occasionally, new and more interesting job opportunities came up, but, senses slightly dulled, the colleague never applied for them. Consequently, they were filled by those that the colleague didn't think quite as good as themselves, and so they drew back another notch, ramped down their effort another degree, downgraded their enthusiasm another level. And then, unexpectedly, the business they worked for was sold – but only the assets, and they were, suddenly, without a job. It seemed like (and perhaps was) an existential crisis. But with the help of former colleagues that person ended up at one of the Big 4 accounting firms – where, all of a sudden, they had to prove themselves all over again. Freed from the shackles of their own torpor, something remarkable happened. They became ambitious again, and grabbed not just the opportunities given them, but more besides, and built up a practice that now also provides employment to others. Ambition rekindled, inspiration and creativity flowed – the positive energy of ambition, rather than the negative energy of acedia. And properly handled, who wouldn't choose the former over the latter? In a race between ambition and acedia there can only be one way to run, only one prize, only one winner.

Ambition: without adjectives

Something creative; a desire to make work better (more relevant, productive, even more profitable); to bring movement into a life, rather than stasis: those can all be "ambition", but shorn of its unattractive adjectives. How do we get there, though, how do we drive those unattractive connotations away? Well, let's think about our ambitious colleague and the new initiative they are launching. There are a number of angles to pursue. Why are they doing it? For selfish or altruistic reasons? For personal gain, or public good? Some mix of those (and many more)? What is it that they are trying to do? Is it "transformational" (= big, disruptive) or incremental? Does it affect lots of people, or just them? And how do they do it? Do they work with others, exchanging ideas? Or do they work on their own, perhaps acquiring other people's ideas as they go along? From even this brief set of questions, the basic point re-emerges that "ambition" cannot be narrowly defined; it is, rather, a range of possibilities around growth and activity that can be accomplished and achieved in different ways.

Being the Good Samaritan: showing mercy

So, back to the question of the parable: how do we show mercy to our ambitious colleague? Perhaps they are consumed by their "ambition" (the desire for wealth, or public recognition, or power). Perhaps that drags them away from family, from friends, from themselves, and from God. Perhaps they justify it as just one more year of hard work, just one more successful deal, just one more promotion, just one more large annual bonus, and then they'll quit.

But let me stop there, because in this list of all the things that may be going wrong, there is more than a hint of judgment on our part. We may think the remedy for this ambition is a no-nonsense, shape-up lecture (or, perhaps, a sermon). But that is not what mercy is about. As we noted in the last chapter, the Good Samaritan knows nothing of, and does not enquire about, the injured man. There is no investigation and no judgment. Mercy is something different – leading primarily to healing, perhaps, rather than reformation. We need to tread carefully.

How, then, can we truly show mercy while also avoiding gorging on the delicious fruit of disapproval? There are all the obvious (if not particularly easy) ways: very gently, gradually, non-judgmentally talking to the person, and trying to get inside their motivation – which in fact means mostly listening rather than talking. What makes them seek affirmation and success? Is there current unhappiness at work; unhappiness in their personal life; is there disappointment from earlier in their career that still rankles or embarrasses; was there some childhood failure that caused a withholding of approval or withdrawal of affection? Why do they think that what they are pursuing ambitiously will make them happier, or better liked, or more highly thought of? And have they considered the effect it will have on other people – and also on them? These are questions totally worth asking, and answers to which we should listen very carefully. But that perhaps deals with only half the issue, and on its own might simply fall in the category of either blocking or mitigating the effects of ambition. If, however, we're looking to draw a contrast between ambition and acedia, between movement and listlessness, then perhaps a second, and more fruitful, element can be added by taking Paul's analogy and working it through a little more.

Paul does not deny the presence – or usefulness – of ambition. As a runner runs to win, and trains hard to reach that goal, so should we focus and refine our ambition. But to what end? Paul says – not disapprovingly – that the athlete seeks a winner's crown that will not last. But he goes on to add that we should seek an everlasting crown. Paul had a certain objective in mind for the Christians of Corinth,[4] but how might we repurpose this for the workplace – the workplace about which God cares deeply?[5] Well not, I would argue, by setting up a stark dichotomy between bad "earthly" ambition, and good "heavenly" ambition. To your average colleague, that might seem much closer to condemnation than to mercy; an impossible choice, with unappealing outcomes. But instead, how about making the race for the earthly and the heavenly crowns the same (or, at least, more similar)? Put in a different way, can we make our colleague's self-interest converge with something that is also good for others? There's the old cliché of "doing well, by doing good", but if the CEO, CFO, the HR manager, and all those other characters above can be steered from our first set of examples towards our second set, then the business as well as the individuals will do well. To want to succeed is not a failing. The way in which we do that, however, and the amount of benefit we bring to others can be.

To illustrate one way this convergence between self-interest and common good might happen, I want to use

---

4   Avoiding continued pagan practices around food, and avoiding factionalism within the church.

5   It is worth mentioning the idea of Miroslav Volf, referred to in *Where is God at Work?* (Monarch, 2015). Volf argues that we are called to be co-workers with God in the workplace, helping Him heal in that place one small piece of the wounded creation that will be perfected at the end of time – a healing facilitated by loving our neighbour, our colleague.

another example from my first boss at GE. It's an example that ties in well with the opening passage from Corinthians, because he would always say that he never hired people to fill particular slots; he "simply" hired the best "athletes" and they then figured out what needed to be done. But his genius didn't so much lie in hiring the athletes (good though they were), as in how he structured the department, welding us into a team. As I make clear in a subsequent chapter, he did not micro-manage. But what he did do was to ensure that the ambitions of his employees (people who, in a law firm for example, could have been structurally opposed to each other) were aligned in working together for the good of the whole tax department, and our client, the company. To slightly restate this, he structured the department – workflow, as well as compensation, reward, and recognition – so that our ambitions were channelled towards a common goal through teamwork, rather than into a set of individual goals. In that way, the ambition that could have been a destructive force, became a largely positive force that pulled people together rather than apart. So, in contrast to my early days at my law firm, what could have been a zero-sum situation where there was a loser for every winner, became a situation where if you won then everyone won. And indeed, the ambition of one person to make the team better could inspire – rather than suppress or depress – the ambitions of the others. What is true for a tax department can, of course, be equally true for a sales team or a research department. Ambition channelled into teamwork can be not just commercially and financially rewarding, but also rewarding in the relationships that are formed and support that is offered.

So, showing mercy to our ambitious colleague will involve neither strenuous criticism nor walking away/crossing over to the other side of the road. It involves stopping with that colleague, trying to find out what it is that motivates them (and is injuring them), and then working with them. But working with them not to turn them into a saint (or even a model of humility) but very gently steering – subverting, perhaps – their ambition into a place where it becomes also a gift, a benefit for others. Working in a team for the common good to achieve the truly advantageous merger; the more appropriately valued company; the better nurtured employees; the unproductive spending diverted to more productive ends; a safer, healthier workplace. Working with that colleague, however difficult they might seem, to achieve a better end, a healing.

Being the injured man: accepting mercy

When it comes to accepting mercy, it may well be that the unhealthy ambition that we spot so clearly in others, we completely fail to see in ourselves. And, therefore, our accepting mercy may involve us allowing our colleagues to help us temper our own damaging ambition. But, equally, in light of what we have been discussing, there is the real possibility that the mercy we need to accept from our ambitious colleague is to have more, rather than less, ambition. We may be lying in the road injured by our proud, arrogant, blind ambition; but we may also be lying there, injured by our total lack of ambition.

But how could making us more ambitious be viewed as merciful? Well, think again of the spiritual and mental deadness that comes with the lack of ambition – the early church's acedia – that increasing disengagement with our work, and our surroundings, and our fellow humans. If it were put that bluntly to us, all of us would deny that we suffer that sort of lack of ambition. But put it slightly differently, and it becomes more plausible. Perhaps you tell yourself that you'll just play it safe in these tricky times because you need the job; or that it's dangerous to experiment because of a mercurial boss; or that you're coping with so much outside of work that you just need to ease back a little at work. For these, and for 101 other reasons and rationalizations, you don't stretch yourself. You do what's required of you, but no more. You settle into a comfortable routine. You're clear in your own mind that you're not failing and that yes, one day soon, maybe, you'll try to hit the home run. But those days that you wait before acting can have a habit of becoming months; and months becoming years; and what was temporary becomes permanent. This does no harm, you tell yourself, because, after all, if you don't try you can't fail, right? But where's the spark – where's the Holy Spirit in all this? Ambition doesn't have to be grandiose. It doesn't have to be earth-shattering. It doesn't even have to be "ambition" if we don't like the word. But a desire to grow, to fulfil our own potential, to change things for the better, both for us and for others in even the smallest way in the context in which we work (junior or senior; young or old), is life-giving. In a very real sense, if we stop growing then we begin to diminish.

Of course, accepting this mercy often sounds easier in theory than it may be in practice. I was certainly challenged from time to time in all the law firms in which I worked to show more ambition. But the work didn't feel essential to me, not life-affirming, not my calling if you will, so I did just enough (although the minimum of 2,000 billable hours generally felt like more than "just enough"). But I knew something wasn't right. The stimulation that I had received at school, and especially at university, was missing and I didn't see that this type of work would ever replace that for me. So, while I took pleasure in things outside of work, and friendships within, at the heart of the experience was acedia. That deadening feeling that the next forty years might look like this – survival, but not much more. However, I had no real idea how to break out of the vicious circle. And then, thankfully, my hand was forced.[6] I could have gone to another firm, and found a slightly safer berth doing much the same. But I didn't. To use Miroslav Volf's language, knowing that something was not right, I worked with the Holy Spirit to determine what my true charism might be – the thing that I could do best, where I could use the gifts I had been given to the advantage of God, and others (and, to be sure, also myself). Or, to put that in secular language: I rediscovered the ambition to do something worthwhile that would challenge me; that would make me grow; that would make me feel alive again. And then I tried to figure out how to get there. But that challenge to be more ambitious, to break free from the grip of acedia – wherever it came from – was truly mercy.

---

6   As readers of the chapter on "The P45/Pink Slip" in *Where is God at Work?* will remember.

3

THE INCOMPETENT COLLEAGUE

"Then the kingdom of heaven will be like this.
Ten bridesmaids took their lamps and went
to meet the bridegroom. Five of them were
foolish, and five were wise. When the foolish
took their lamps, they took no oil with them;
but the wise took flasks of oil with their lamps.
As the bridegroom was delayed, all of them
became drowsy and slept. But at midnight there
was a shout, 'Look! Here is the bridegroom!
Come out to meet him.' Then all those
bridesmaids got up and trimmed their lamps.
The foolish said to the wise, 'Give us some of
your oil, for our lamps are going out.' But the
wise replied, 'No! There will not be enough for
you and for us; you had better go to the dealers
and buy some for yourselves.' And while they
went to buy it, the bridegroom came, and those
who were ready went with him into the wedding
banquet; and the door was shut. Later the other
bridesmaids came also, saying, 'Lord, lord,
open to us.' But he replied, 'Truly I tell you, I do

not know you.' Keep awake therefore, for you know neither the day nor the hour."
Matthew 25:1–13 NRSV

Although it's thirty years ago now, I still squirm slightly when I think back to some of the things that I got wrong as a trainee lawyer. A couple of incidents particularly stick in my mind. In my first week, I was sent out to help close a large property transaction. I had no (absolutely no) idea what I was doing. After floundering around for a time, the lawyer on the other side of the transaction took pity on me, and walked me through the transaction papers, pointing out what I should be looking for. Some months later, after about a year at the firm, I spent three months training in the tax department. The technical nature of tax work, unfortunately, made any blunders much more obvious. Very early on I was asked to do some work for a prestigious stockbroker on a foreign stock listing. Suffice it to say, I missed a critical point (only one?), and much of the work had to be redone. This resulted only in a fairly restrained note from the client saying how nice it would be the next time to have someone who knew what they were doing working on these matters; and an equally restrained note from one of the senior tax partners to the rest of the department, saying how nice it would be the next time to check with them before giving this type of advice. I felt pretty small (and useless).

But the all-time worst was a long Friday afternoon meeting with a highly entrepreneurial new client who was disposing of a business. The commercial partner who normally dealt with that client had been called away, and my tax partner was busy. The stand-in commercial partner was the nicest of people, but definitely not at their sharpest after lunch (and especially not after Friday lunch). And I was (as usual) way out of my depth on the relative advantages of stock sales vs asset sales.

Eventually, after several hours of the client being required to explain the facts again and again to the commercial partner, and my unhelpful near-silence to almost every question posed, the client exploded, screaming: "For God's sake! Just go and get me somebody competent!" Not needing to hear the invitation twice, I flew upstairs, found my tax partner – who was just leaving for the weekend – and managed to persuade/beg them to come and sort it out. (As you can tell, these early years were a fruitful period for humbling experiences.)

Reacting to incompetence

There is nothing quite like incompetence at work – whether the colleague is the boss, or a teammate, or a direct report – to spark the full range of negative emotions. Like a ripple in a pond – or, perhaps, a bad odour – the effects of incompetence seem to spread out in every direction. Fellow workers have to do the work not done, or clear up the mess by redoing the work done badly the first time. The client or customer often suffers through shoddy goods or services – and a reduced trust and confidence in that business (or, perhaps, in business more generally). The business itself may suffer through reduced profits, or reputation, or both. If the person is also a boss, the effects may spread wider, out from the actual work of the business, into bad management of processes and procedures which causes dissatisfaction and resentment among the employees. How often – whether at a fellow worker, or your boss, or a client, or a customer – have you felt like screaming: "Just go and get me somebody competent"?

We are used to hearing from Jesus about the forgiveness we must show, and the second chances we must give, so there is something comfortingly and affirmingly censorious about the parable of the wise and the foolish bridesmaids (or "virgins" in

King James, and the original Greek). Here, all ten were given fair warning of what was coming: five were competent/wise/sensible and five were incompetent/foolish/silly. When the messenger announces that the bridegroom is about to arrive, the five incompetent bridesmaids beg for lamp oil from the competent ones; but, instead of a Sermon-on-the-Mount style storyline that leads to a heart-warming ending about the competent five sharing their oil (or even giving it all away), the incompetent five are sent away with a flea in their ear to rouse the local lamp oil dealer… at midnight. By the time they get back to the wedding venue, the groom has gone in and the doors are closed. When they beg to be let in, the bridegroom replies robustly that he does not even know them. And so, at last, it appears, the incompetent get their just deserts. "If only that happened at work…" you might be thinking.

What is incompetence?

We'll return to the parable later, but first it might be helpful to look a little harder at the word "incompetence" itself. Obviously, and literally, it means a lack of competence, although it does get broadened out sometimes to include other issues with similar effects (such as laziness, which we'll look at separately in a later chapter). But not all incompetence is the same, because there can be not only several quite distinct causes, but also a couple of different types. So, let's analyse a couple of examples from my law firm stories above:

- Incompetence can be caused by simple inexperience. This type of incompetence can itself be further subdivided. The inexperience may arise because you simply do not yet know the full body of technical rules that you need to master in order to be able to give the professional advice, or perform the operation, or manufacture the piece of equipment. Or you may have that technical knowledge, but don't yet have enough practice or experience in a pressured setting to execute on that technical knowledge. That certainly fits the first of the stories I told, where I had neither knowledge nor experience.

- Incompetence can also arise in situations where those skills or rules have been incorrectly or imperfectly learned; or where the mechanics – the practicalities of how to put that knowledge into operation, how to put that knowledge to work – have been badly learned. To be sure, that may be laziness or arrogance ("I can't be bothered… or don't have to be bothered. How hard can it be?"). But there can be other reasons, too. People's minds work in different ways. Some can learn, absorb, and then successfully deploy a large body of complex rules. Others can't. And however hard you may try, forcing a round peg (me) in a square hole (technical tax rules) is never going to work, and, in this context, will produce only incompetence.

- Finally, incompetence can sometimes arise because of circumstances unrelated to our level of knowledge, skill, and application (or lack thereof). It can arise, for example, from simple overload. We really only do have time to do five tasks, but we are required to do ten. The only way we can achieve that target is by cutting corners on all ten. There can be differing reasons for this overload – we may do it to ourselves (I'll also look at that in another chapter), or there may be a systemic problem at work, such as unreasonable and/or unrealistic targets. Or deadlines, for any number of reasons, may be too short. Or the issue may simply not be technically solvable. But, in each case, the outcome will be (or will look like) incompetence.

In all of these cases (certainly in mine), we usually know – more or less – that we are incompetent. Put slightly differently, even as we plough on, we know, at least vaguely, what we don't know. But there is a different type of incompetence, where we feel incorrectly (sometimes recklessly) that we do have the knowledge or skill to deal with a situation. In that case, perhaps our self-confidence outstrips our ability; perhaps it is skill we once had, but has now faded for one reason or another. I'll look at this more in the chapter on our arrogant colleague, but we can also see this type of incompetence in many cases in the workplace, from the very top of the organization right to the bottom.

In the workplace, as elsewhere, a number of different issues may gather under the general heading of incompetence. The reasons may be individual or institutional; may reflect a lack of skill, a lack of experience, or bad procedures. But the effect is much the same: work gets done badly; the workplace is diminished.

What's going on in the parable?

I want to return to the wise and foolish bridesmaids for a moment. In this parable Jesus is doing a number of things, but enabling us to condemn incompetence is probably not among them. So, let's look a little harder. Set in a section of Matthew's Gospel that deals with the issue of when Jesus will return, of when the Second Coming will occur, this parable is trying to do a couple of important things: first, to explain in everyday language that the bridegroom (Jesus) has been delayed, but that He will be coming; and second, to explain how we should prepare for that arrival during that time of waiting. With both of those in mind, it would be totally contrary to the gospel of freely offered salvation (and love) if we were encouraged to think that we can only get to heaven through our own "wise" efforts, and/or through withholding whatever we may have from our neighbours in need. So, how then to make sense of this story, and to discover its applicability to the workplace?

In fact, the parable is completely consistent with a gospel that tells us again and again that we are quite capable of injuring ourselves by cutting ourselves off from the love of God and refusing His gift of healing and reconciliation. Looked at in that way, the parable is no longer an invitation to criticize incompetence and act selfishly in the face of another's carelessness. It is about being the best we can be, including through proper preparation, and the difficulty (on occasion, impossibility) of rectifying that lack of preparation once the action has started. And that suggests a different role for us as Christians and neighbours in the workplace. We do not step into the shoes of the (on a literal reading) censorious bridegroom. Nor do we sit demurely (and, probably, smugly) as one of the five wise bridesmaids on our way to the wedding banquet, watching our incompetent colleagues recede into the darkness. Rather, we have to become a channel for the narrator of the story – Jesus – and help to prevent our fellow workers from finding themselves in the position where an expected event occurs at an unexpected time, at which point they discover they do not have enough metaphorical lamp oil for the task in hand.

Being the Good Samaritan: showing mercy

How we can be the neighbour – how we can show "mercy" – to our incompetent colleague? The parable of the bridesmaids offers, I believe, three possibilities. The first relates to what we can do before the event; the second to what we can do at the time of the event; and the third to what we should do after the event.

Showing mercy: before

In relation to the time before the event, if the parable of the bridesmaids is indeed about the importance of preparation, then the application to the workplace is fairly clear. In the first few stories that I told about my early days as a lawyer, my problem was a threefold lack of knowledge, training, and experience. There was no way after only a few days in the job that I could be expected to know what to do at a closing, or how to handle a significant matter for a major client without fairly close supervision. And this is important because it can have effects well beyond just that single incident. While some of my colleagues found these types of high-wire experiences relatively invigorating, others had their confidence totally shattered and withdrew from the profession almost before they had begun. And that latter result was good for neither the business nor the individual – nor for God's interest in either.

In my case, some supervision and training largely solved that problem. So, before we send someone out solo, or give them the big job, we should ensure that our fellow workers are properly equipped and trained to do the thing that they are being asked to do. That might be formal training, or informal mentoring; it might be showing someone how to do something under supervision a few times, or allowing them to shadow you as you do your job. And it may also include special or intensive training for those who find certain tasks more difficult. In other words, you show mercy by ensuring that your colleague, your neighbour, knows what lamp oil is for, how they use it, and how much they will need. Then when the bridegroom (the event or the transaction) arrives you will have helped your potentially incompetent colleague to be, instead, your competent colleague – thus also helping the workplace, yourself, and God.

Showing mercy: during

Next, how does the parable of the bridesmaids speak to what we should do in the office at the moment that the incompetence manifests itself? (Although, of course, the "moment" may be a series of events, or continuous performance over a period of time.) "Aha," some of you will be saying, "that's easy: they've made their bed, and now they can lie in it. We are not obliged to help them, especially not at a cost to ourselves." Putting aside why we would imagine for a moment that we'd be welcome in the kingdom with that lack of generosity, I don't think that's quite right even within the terms of the parable. Look again at the story. Read literally, it's true that if the wise bridesmaids had shared their oil then none of the ten could have lit their lamps. But if the five had had enough oil for the others, would they have been justified in not sharing? Of course not. Partly because of our general obligation to love our neighbour; but also because of our role as co-worker with God in the workplace. And often we do have enough of that "oil" to share – it is grouchiness rather than scarcity that makes us unwilling to share it. There may indeed be times when we are working so flat-out, or at such a delicate point in a task or transaction, that we really, genuinely, don't have time to help our colleague who has messed up. But, if we're being honest, those times are quite rare. Usually – annoying, time-consuming, or frustrating though it may be – we can find the time to help our incompetent colleague. And in doing that, we help not only them, but also the workplace. We will be the neighbour to our incompetent colleague at the moment of crisis by showing mercy and sharing some of our lamp oil (despite those visceral emotions that will often tempt us in the opposite direction).

Showing mercy: after

And, finally, how does the parable speak to what mercy might be after the event? (Which, again, may be the end of a series of events and period of time – perhaps at an annual performance review.) Here I think I have to be a bit careful, otherwise one aspect of what follows will sound very much like slamming the door of the wedding feast in the face of the foolish bridesmaids. But before we get to that, if the "incompetence" was caused by lack of experience or training, then that takes us back to the first lesson from the parable, namely that supervision and training are important. Likewise, if the incompetence was caused by a completely uncharacteristic mistake, then mercy would dictate a second chance.

Showing mercy: when competence can never be achieved

But the tough case comes when it is clear that someone is "incompetent" because they can't do the job – and will never be able to. They simply do not have, and will never be able to acquire, the necessary skills and capability for that job. Here I would argue that it is not neighbourly, not merciful, to keep someone in a job which they are not able to do. It's not merciful to the fellow workers who are constantly having to share their lamp oil, and it's not good for the business itself. The CEO when I joined GE was the legendary manager Jack Welch. One of his stated management techniques was to dismiss the bottom ten per cent of workers each year. (Although it never worked that harshly in practice.) His rationale was that if they weren't up to the job, then they should be helped to find one that they could do, rather than feel trapped in one they couldn't. To be trapped in that way was bad for the business and it was ultimately bad for them.

As I've written before, there is, of course, a lot of tension associated with losing a job; but there's also a lot associated with holding on to one that you can't do.[7] Doing a job where you always seem to be messing up is incredibly stressful. You feel you are hanging on by your fingertips; the sword of discipline/redundancy/disaster is always dangling above you, hanging only by a single thread. The mercy in this case would be to get the colleague out of that job and into one which they can handle, or even excel at. For example, in the last of the three stories that I told at the start of the chapter, mercy to the partner was not to keep sending them to meetings where people screamed, "Just go and get me somebody competent!" at them. It would have been (and eventually was) early retirement. But that was not to shut them out of the wedding feast because they had failed. It was to remove the partner from a situation where they could only ever fail, time and again – and, hopefully, to put them in one where they might succeed.

Miroslav Volf makes the point that while every job is godly, and worthy of respect, that does not mean the job that we are in is the right one for us – ordained by God – and that to leave it if it is not right for us would be to offend the Creator. In fact, we should be working with the Holy Spirit to determine the job that is truly our calling. Accordingly, if we can offer our incompetent colleague a way out of this dead end, to something and somewhere where they can again feel they are holding their own, contributing, adding value, then that truly is mercy – much more so than keeping them just about patched up in a job they cannot (and know they cannot) really do.

---

7 I used to have a relatively regular nightmare, where I would dream that someone walked into my office one day and said, "Enough of all this policy work. That's just fluff. You're going to start doing real tax again." Which, of course, I wasn't capable of doing… But I needed the job to support my family, and what else was I going to do? I'd actually be thrilled to wake up and see the clock, even if it was 3 a.m., on the basis that I wasn't – at least on that day – going to be forced to start once again covering up my incompetent tracks.

Being the injured man: accepting mercy

In considering whether we are the injured man, the obvious point is that we ourselves may be the incompetent colleague. In the past, as I have made crystal clear, I have been that colleague (and may well still be). In that case, accepting mercy means taking the training and advice that are offered to make me as good as I can be; using those opportunities to nourish my own skills and aptitudes. And it can also mean accepting, as we've just seen, that we are simply not cut out to be in some jobs; that we will always be a drag on our colleagues and on the business (in addition to tormenting ourselves). It can mean accepting from others the merciful message that we should be looking (working with the Spirit) for something to which we are better suited.

But there's another, perhaps counter-intuitive aspect to accepting mercy when we're incompetent. And that's the benefit that lies in realizing that we actually are incompetent. My spiritual adviser[8] once told me that rather than being (or trying to be) in control of everything the whole time, it would be better for me if I went and "stumbled around in the mud" for a while, unable to get out. That sounds a little harsh, but in fact it was both heartfelt and humane; because the downside of "competence" is the illusion of control. The illusion that we, as individuals, divorced from a community, can shape the world around us. The illusion that we as human beings, divorced from God, are the source of our own success. Competence makes us think more highly of ourselves, and makes us forget what we owe to God, and what we owe to others. Incompetence, however, reminds us of those things. If we're staggering about

---

8   Every priest is counselled to have a "spiritual adviser" whom they see on a regular basis. Although advising can, on occasion, involve something close to therapy, the adviser primarily helps the advisee in their spiritual journey: to reflect on where they have been, and discern where it is that God may wish them to go.

in the mud, completely unable to get our footing, to regain our balance, we quickly realize that we need help. We realize we need someone to reach out an arm to steady us; to reach out a hand to pull us up. We remember that we need others, and we need God. We're not self-sufficient, not autonomous, and not that clever. So, recognizing that we are incompetent, and that we do need the help of others, can be mercy indeed.

There's another element to this. The illusion of competence, of being able to do it all, of having almost limitless capability, can lead us into taking on too much and becoming ever busier. On the flip side, however, because we believe the story we tell ourselves, doing less can become associated in our own minds with incompetence. It's a simple formula: competent people (who can) do more; incompetent people (who can't) do less. And we lose a sense of proportion. We'll look at this more in the chapter on the lazy colleague, but I'll just note here that acknowledging that I am incompetent can allow me the opportunity to reassess, regain perspective, and, perhaps, slow down a little and give more time to what really matters – including other people.

Accepting mercy: which bridesmaid are you?

Of course, we should always try to do the best we can, and we should try to be the best we can be. We owe that to ourselves, to our fellow workers, to the business – and to the God who created us. But not in a smug, self-satisfied way. We should not imagine ourselves one of the five wise bridesmaids staring out of the window as their incompetent colleagues are turned away from the feast and sent out into the darkness. This parable – and our lives – are not about how competent we are, and how incompetent others are, with our virtue being rewarded, and their failings being punished. Rather, we need to recognize how "foolish", how incompetent, we really are – and how little in control. And then we should marvel that through the sacrifice of Jesus, the grace of God, and the kindness of others, somehow – somehow – hands reach out to pick us up, arms reach out to steady us. At midnight, in the darkness, despite the fact that we lost our lamp oil and fell asleep – despite all that, the bridegroom holds open the door, the light flooding out, and beckons us to join the feast. Not because we are worthy of it, but because He loves us, incompetent as we truly are.

4

THE SHY COLLEAGUE

"You are the salt of the earth; but if salt has lost its taste, how can its saltiness be restored? It is no longer good for anything, but is thrown out and trampled under foot. You are the light of the world. A city built on a hill cannot be hid. No one after lighting a lamp puts it under the bushel basket, but on the lampstand, and it gives light to all in the house. In the same way, let your light shine before others, so that they may see your good works and give glory to your Father in heaven."

Matthew 5:13–16 NRSV

I began writing this chapter on the way back from an enormous business conference in Turkey. The President and Prime Minister both came to speak, and there were at least a thousand business delegates, as well as assorted central bankers and finance ministers. I had had mixed feelings about going there, and when I arrived the numbers felt overwhelming. I knew exactly four out of those one thousand – and those four had better things to do than hang around with me. Many of the other delegates seemed to know each other. The more that they greeted one another warmly, the less motivated I felt to do anything other than look even more intently at my iPhone. In one of the first sessions, my Turkish neighbour tried to strike up a conversation with me. But we found we had not even single words of a language in common, far less sentences. As others got louder, I got still quieter. At the first coffee break, I used well-honed evasive tactics to avoid contact – moving not so fast as to be noticeably doing continuous circuits of the room, but not so slowly that there was the slightest risk of being stopped by someone who might want to talk. At the end of a long afternoon of incomprehensible speeches (my headphones weren't working) we were reminded, in English, about the gala dinner in the evening. "You've got to be kidding," I thought. "Another three hours of this?" Instead, I jumped on the bus back to the hotel, shut the door, ordered room service, and settled down to a solitary (and – by comparison – relaxing) evening of emails. The whole event reminded me of those awful teenage dances where I didn't like the music, didn't know the people, and looked at my watch every few minutes desperately hoping that time might be moving faster than I knew it ever could.

Yet my perception of myself at that conference is very different to the one that many others have of me more generally. They see me up on the stage presenting on a work topic, or in the pulpit preaching on a religious one. They read the numerous letters that I sign on behalf of various business organizations, or they see me leading large meetings where I try to speak to many of the participants and hold myself open for anyone to talk to me. So, which is it? Am I the shy colleague – or am I the exact opposite? Well, the truthful answer is "it depends", and I hope in this chapter to make a little more sense of that apparent contradiction.

Shyness

The first question we have to answer, however, is a basic one: exactly what is shyness? I think it's important to say straight off that it's not a medical condition (such as depression, which we'll look at later). It's more a collection of character traits. Most dictionary definitions of shy include words such as "timid", "quiet", "reserved", "retiring", "modest", and "diffident". And to those we can add some specifics from my example above: being overwhelmed by crowds; fear of new social situations; feeling an outsider in an established group (from outside the tribe); being an introvert. It's about being quiet, about holding back, and about letting others do the talking. But, some might ask, is that all bad? As we'll discuss when looking at the verbose colleague, too much talking may not always be a huge plus for the workplace either. But that's for another day. The issue here is how shyness may affect the workplace.

The problems with shyness

I would suggest there are two principal issues about shyness in the workplace. The first, and fairly obvious one, is that shyness might hold our colleague back, preventing them from giving the input of which they are capable, and getting the recognition they deserve, as they are crowded out by their less shy colleagues. The second problem, which is perhaps a little less obvious, is the one that the reading from Matthew hints at. Shyness can be us hiding our "light" under a bowl ("bushel" in the King James Version); it can be failing to add our "salt" to people and situations around us. And that impacts not just the person involved, but is also a loss for the workplace and for God's work of creation that is going on there. Put slightly differently, shyness (our own, or others') is not just a personal difficulty, a personal loss; it may also be a communal loss.

Direct effects: on the colleague and on the workplace

I think we all know colleagues (or perhaps it is you?) who through shyness missed out on the opportunity to participate in a key project because they were overlooked; who missed out on promotion because they didn't draw attention to themselves; who missed out on recognition they deserved for the work they'd done because they didn't communicate their involvement or success; or because, slightly more malignly, another colleague stepped in front of them as they hung back and took the credit instead. That's a problem in the workplace – particularly for those which promote themselves as meritocracies – for a number of reasons. It's bad for the shy colleague themselves: they will often feel frustrated, and quite possibly un(or under-)appreciated. That might make them withdraw still further, and/or put less into their job. But it's also bad for the whole office when the system of meritocratic recognition and rewards doesn't work the way it's meant to. It may discourage others; or it might encourage self-seeking (and often unproductive) behaviour in order to gain that recognition.

So, let me tell a story which pulls together a number of these strands. (And, twenty years after the event, I still recall very sharply this example of my own shyness that affected not just me but the work of the office for weeks afterwards.) I was at the US Treasury, and had been working with my boss on a fairly high-level tax project. It had featured in the *Financial Times* and *New York Times* and drawn the ire of the US Senate. Our ultimate boss, the US Treasury Secretary, had supported us, but we had reached an impasse. So, my boss decided to call a meeting of the great and the good of the Washington tax world (as someone originally appointed by JFK, he had real pulling power). All of them were distinguished, and some were living legends (OK, it was tax…). The day of the meeting arrived, and I'd made all the preparations, and lined up all the arguments. I was slightly in awe of the crowd, so I started tentatively. And into the breach jumped a colleague who had done virtually nothing on the project (or much else). Within no time they were acting as though they had driven the project in the near past, and had all the ideas for the near future. It was galling beyond belief, but having let the opportunity slip through shyness, I couldn't exactly storm back into the conversation. So, I sat there seething in the knowledge that, when all these people walked out, they would do so:

- without a true appreciation of who had put in all the work (petty);

- with a much better impression of my colleague than that person deserved (equally petty);

- without truly understanding the complex interaction between all the issues (more serious);

- without, therefore, having been able to give us the advice and guidance we really wanted and needed (very serious).

I spent days not able to figure out whom I was most angry at: myself for not conquering my shyness; my colleague for their opportunism; or my boss for not stopping the charade (as I saw it) and putting the meeting back on a proper footing (i.e. with me in charge). I got over my annoyance relatively quickly, but the project was set back, and my relationship with that colleague was never the same again.

So, the shy colleague – and those they work with – can be disadvantaged, even damaged by shyness. People do not contribute (or are not able to contribute) as they should. Productivity, effectiveness, morale all suffer. But there's more to it, I think, than just individual or collective hurt, and more to it than just the bottom-line effects.

Indirect effects: losing salt and light

We have talked before about the opportunity to use our talents to the best of our abilities at work to participate in the healing of God's creation through the improvement of the workplace. But that's not just the opportunity to improve the physical infrastructure and productivity (truly interested though God is in that); and not just the opportunity to help our neighbour. It's also about the potential of the workplace to be an example that others may recognize and wish to adopt themselves, both inside and outside the business. And this is where the idea of "salt and light" in this chapter's opening Bible passage comes in.

Jesus' words come from the beginning of the Sermon on the Mount, just after the Beatitudes ("blessed are the poor in spirit..."), and they are addressed specifically to the disciples: to the life they are to lead, and to the influence their example is to have on others around them. Salt enhances taste and preserves food; light enables us to see around ourselves and makes things clear. Jesus is telling the disciples that they are to bring distinctiveness to the life of the people, the community around them, by living out the life that He is teaching them about. Put slightly differently, they (and we) are to add to the life of others by being salt which enhances those other people's lives, and allows them to appreciate those lives more; and by being light which will enable other people to see more clearly what is right and wrong, and how they can find fulfilment as well as forgiveness.

But while this is a call to the disciples (and us) as individuals, by action and example, to be salt and light to others, equally importantly it is also a call to groups of Christians – the church – to be a community which influences other communities. This community that is called to be salt and light to others is the "city on the hill" in the opening Scripture verses.[9] Individuals through their own actions can have a very strong, positive effect on other people's lives and on the lives of communities. But the effect and example that can follow from a group of people – a community – living together harmoniously and lovingly, is slightly different from the effect an individual can have. That's because being good on our own is different from being good together; and being a good community is different from being simply a collection of good individuals. Individuals do not themselves make a society – communities do. And although we will go to heaven one by one, our lives will be better, more fulfilled, and almost certainly more faithful, as the members of a healthy, caring community, than they would be as a collection of atomized individuals. So, we are called upon both as individuals in the workplace (neighbours) as well as the part of the community that is the workplace (neighbourhood) to be an example to others. To be salt, to be the light on the stand, to be the city on the hill.

But for both the community (city) and individual (lamp), the light will only be effective if it shines and illuminates; the salt will only be effective in adding taste and distinctiveness if it is mixed with food. Therefore, light under a bushel will not be light for these purposes; and salt that is kept in a barrel might as well be without taste because it can have no effect. To bring this back to our central point about shyness in the workplace, as either an individual or a community, however

---

9   This is a metaphor with particular resonance in the US, from the time of its first use by John Winthrop in the mid-seventeenth century, to its use by Ronald Reagan in the late twentieth. It is now somewhat associated with American "exceptionalism", but is (when stripped of that political context) a call to all of us to be, by example, an inspiration to those around us; to be a bright illumination of the faith that burns within us.

"good" we are, whatever potential we have to be a shining example to others of how to live a good life well, and work for God's creation in the workplace, that will never progress beyond mere potential if shyness prevents us from sharing that salt and light with others.

And these limiting effects of shyness can manifest themselves in many ways. So, for example, shyness might prevent us from reaching out to our fellow workers in need: from reaching out to those who are physically ill or worn out; from reaching out to those in troubled relationships with family or with friends; to those embarrassed by past actions, or those who are the subject of vicious gossip. If shyness prevents us from reaching out to them, from truly engaging with them, then all our good thoughts and good intentions remain simply potential – light under the bowl. And, likewise, if shyness prevents us not just advocating for ideas that will make our business more productive and more efficient, but also prevents our business from being a supportive and nourishing community for all its workers, or prevents it from being an example to other businesses (through its treatment of employees, customers, suppliers, the local community), then all our good intentions remain simply potential – salt with no taste. To be very clear, shyness, something many are born with or bred into, is not in any way a fault, far less a "sin". But, in certain circumstances, it is something that we are called to overcome for our own good and for the good of those around us.

One last word on this: we can be good as individuals, or as a community, and inspire others to follow our example, all without any reference to our faith – and the world will still be a much better place for it. But the true salt and light – the defining brightness, and the sharpness of taste – comes when we make clear our motivation as Christians. Not only does it enable us to be salt and light in good times and bad, in difficult times and easy ones, but it demonstrates to others that it is the constant love of God that impels us to be these things, and to carry on doing them. As we've discussed before, this doesn't mean preaching by the water cooler, or passing out pamphlets in the neighbouring cubicles. But it can mean gently, respectfully – but unmistakably – letting others know the source of our inspiration and ability to carry on trying to help, day after day.

Being the Good Samaritan: showing mercy

Showing mercy: running meetings

To come to the practicalities, there are some fairly obvious ways of being the Good Samaritan to a shy colleague. You can try to help their confidence by, for example, seeking to improve their communication skills through training or personal mentoring. You can make sure they get the credit they deserve when they do have a good idea. You can make sure that you let introverts know that you understand that they need some time to be quiet and recharge their batteries, while also encouraging them to understand that they will need to speak out at other times. You can make sure that meetings are structured in such a way that everyone is allowed to contribute, not just the loud and the pushy. While that may sound easy, until I had to try to do it myself I had never understood how difficult, and yet how vital, it was to have a chair of a meeting/committee/group who was both totally unobtrusive and very firm.

So, I have learned to gently cut people off by saying: "So, if I can just summarize your thoughts..." I have learned to say, even when it's clear that people have not finished: "This has been really interesting/valuable/insightful, but we have to move on…" And I have also learned to be blunt – but never personal, I hope – and say: "I'm really sorry, but our job is to get through the agenda, so let's move on…" I always try to make sure that it's not about me; but I also always make clear who is running the meeting. And I believe that that combination of unobtrusiveness and firmness, in so many settings, can really ensure that everyone gets their say (and moment in the sun), while at the same time also ensuring that no one, be they shy or loquacious/verbose, feels they have been short-changed.

Showing mercy: being salt and light

All of these are relatively obvious (if not always easily achieved), and will be good for the colleague as well as for the workplace. But, to the point I mentioned above, there's nothing identifiably Christian about them. So, the salt and light will become saltier and brighter if we can make clear – gently, yes, but also unmistakeably – our Christian motivation. There are a couple of reasons for this. The first is that in helping someone when we don't need to, when we cross over the road to their side, we will earn their gratitude and most likely also their trust. If we can make clear the love of Christ, then they will note that and may well be receptive to it. More salt and light. Second, if the word gets around as to what we have done, and why we did it, then the community may receive more salt and light. Perhaps it inspires others to act in the same way; perhaps it inspires some to find out more about the faith that motivates us; and perhaps our own work community can inspire other communities. But whichever of those it might be, it is not just our individual colleague who is helped, but the whole community. The light shines a little brighter in (and from) the city on the hill.

Being the injured man: accepting mercy

The most obvious point about accepting mercy is that if we are the shy colleague, then we should willingly accept the help, mentoring, and training which will make us more effective co-workers with God in the workplace, and will make us contributors of salt and light to the community of that workplace. We should not avoid the fact that God sometimes needs us to move beyond our comfort zone, and we should not resent those who are prepared to help us.

But I want to look a little more at a slightly less obvious way in which shyness may leave us injured and in need of mercy. Sometimes our shyness – the silence, not venturing an opinion, holding back when others rush forward – is motivated not so much by timidity, bashfulness, or reserve, as it is by fear allied with pride that makes us not want to appear stupid. Or it may be motivated by a desire to not be held to blame in case anything goes wrong. Or it may be motivated by laziness which means we aren't properly prepared and aren't capable of following through. We'll deal with the last of those in another chapter, but the first two are also important, as I hope the following story may illustrate.

I once had a colleague whose favourite motto was "a fool only betrays themselves by opening their mouth". This colleague was smart, and, in private, funny and engaging. But in every meeting or other setting where a decision needed to be made they would never utter a word. Only at, or close to, the end, having heard everyone else speak, would they offer a non-opinion which repeated back, verbatim, the statements of others. I tackled my colleague on it once, and they admitted freely that they were concerned that they might be thought stupid amid a crowd of very smart people (they wouldn't have been). Furthermore, they freely admitted to an element of risk aversion which grew with each passing year; a fear (phobia, increasingly) of being wrong on a huge issue to the company. "If I don't do anything," they said, "then I can't be wrong." And so that colleague hid behind a mask of shyness, contributing little, slowly atrophying, visibly shrinking.

Accepting mercy: being prepared to fail

The point is that if the shyness that holds people back and diminishes the workplace, is in a sense self-indulgent or even selfish, then we are both seriously damaging ourselves, as well as truly hiding light under a bowl, and taking all the taste out of salt. How? Well, there is the indisputable (if occasionally discomforting) fact that we often learn much more from our failures than our successes. If we never venture a view, if we never contribute, then to be sure we may never fail – but, without question, nor will we really ever have succeeded. To grow, we need to take risks; to learn, we have to be prepared to fail. If we wrap ourselves in cotton wool, however comforting and secure that may seem in the short term, in fact we are short-changing ourselves; short-changing the community to which we should be salt and light (rather than bland monochrome); and short-changing the God in whose image we are made.

So, as the injured man, accepting mercy in this case would be accepting that, despite our fear, God wants us to participate – and that He will love us as much when we fail as when we succeed, whatever those around us may say. Accepting mercy in this case is understanding that God wants us to try whether we succeed or fail, because even if we fail, it is in the act of trying that we will still add that distinctive salt and light to the community. Accepting mercy in this case is understanding, as Paul did, that however ridiculous some might think us, we add salt and light by "speaking as a fool… by boast[ing] of the things that show [our] weakness… So [we] will boast all the more gladly of [our] weaknesses … for whenever [we are] weak, then [we are] strong" (2 Corinthians 11:21, 30; 12:9, 10 NRSV). God doesn't want us to hold back, always playing the safety card, always trying to avoid trouble. God, rather, wants us always to try, not necessarily always (or perhaps not even often) to succeed, but really just to try.

I want to close with the conference that I described at the beginning of this chapter. I was there because I had agreed to chair a panel discussion on tax and cross-border investment in large infrastructure projects with a senior development banker, a top international tax official, and a leading businessman. It was the first time this business organization had dealt with tax. It gave me the opportunity to demonstrate that business was a constructive player in the process. And it allowed me to build up contacts that might lead to further discussions in the future. If all went well, this might play a (very small) role in encouraging much-needed investment in developing countries, which would lead to economic growth, more and better-paying jobs, more tax revenue, and stronger societies. So, whatever I might have been feeling on the inside, I put on my game-face, was upbeat, tried to prevent any lengthy silences, and encouraged the others on the panel not just to speak but to stretch themselves a little in their thinking. Afterwards I milled around, chatting to the audience, initiating conversations, handing out my business card, and telling people to contact me with questions, thoughts, anything with which I could help. In another setting, I wouldn't have dreamed of doing this. I would not have dreamed of doing it the day before when I had no role, and no specific task to fulfil. But, when the occasion called for it, I tried, in a very small way, to put aside my "shyness" and participate in a process that might result in something good. Accepting mercy, I tried to be the salt and the light I know that, sometimes very uncomfortably, I am called to be.

5

THE LAZY COLLEAGUE

Now we command you, beloved, in the name of our Lord Jesus Christ, to keep away from believers who are living in idleness and not according to the tradition that they received from us. For you yourselves know how you ought to imitate us; we were not idle when we were with you, and we did not eat anyone's bread without paying for it; but with toil and labour we worked night and day, so that we might not burden any of you. This was not because we do not have that right, but in order to give you an example to imitate. For even when we were with you, we gave you this command: Anyone unwilling to work should not eat. For we hear that some of you are living in idleness, mere busybodies, not doing any work. Now such persons we command and exhort in the Lord Jesus Christ to do their work quietly and to earn their own living. Brothers and sisters, do not be weary in doing what is right. Take note of those who do not obey what we say in this letter; have nothing to do with them, so that they may be ashamed.

Do not regard them as enemies, but warn
them as believers.
2 Thessalonians 3:6–15 NRSV

After two years of working as a trainee lawyer in London, I was offered the opportunity to go to law school in the United States for a year. Still not quite knowing what I wanted to be when I grew up, I had jumped at the opportunity to be a student again. As a history undergraduate in the UK, I'd had a reputation among my contemporaries for being a fairly hard worker. While I'd attended no more lectures than anyone else (none in my second year, to be absolutely precise), I had generally gone to the library for five mornings a week, and always produced my weekly paper without the drama of an "essay crisis". The rest of the time I'd read novels, or cooked, or talked politics, or played bridge (badly). The terms were short, and while I'd taken a paying job in the summers, in the other breaks I'd read still more novels. After two years of "real work" I was looking forward to a return to this entirely congenial life of the mind.[10]

The law school I was going to in the States had an excellent reputation, but was also known for being the least pressured amongst its pressurized peers. I was, therefore, more than a little surprised when I arrived to find that during the long terms/semesters everyone seemed to spend almost all of their time in the library. There were people there in the middle of the night, and throughout the weekends; the daily rush for coveted semi-private reading spaces was a model of frenzied competition; and, if a lecturer specified ten cases to be discussed at the next lecture, then people would read each case from beginning to end, however long it might take them. One

---

10 It should be said this congeniality had been further enhanced in those years by virtue of the fact that the experience had been largely paid for by the taxpayer.

of the more cooperative endeavours was for a group of students to get together and divide up a lecture course into a number of blocks, with each student then producing a summary of their allocated block for the rest of the group. The product varied, but most commonly the "summary" notes would be an almost verbatim record of the lectures. As the year went by, a couple of things struck me: first, it became more and more clear that my undergraduate contemporaries and I had not worked terribly hard at our studies at university; but, second, that the opposite of the negative "lazy" might not be a simple, virtuous "busy". That the appropriate reaction to laziness might be something more than additional activity; something more than what might be undiscriminating "busy-ness".

In an earlier chapter, we looked at acedia, that lassitude or lethargy that leads to a withdrawal from the world and from relationships; a lack of motivation. Acedia carries problems of its own, but it is – to me, at least – distinguished from laziness (or "sloth") by the active choice involved in the latter. In laziness, often a positive decision is made to do nothing. It isn't losing interest in the present and future, so much as positively deciding to do nothing, to freeload, to let others take the strain. The fault ("sin" to some, because "sloth" – but not acedia – made the final cut from the "Eight Thoughts" to the "Seven Deadly Sins")[11] lies in the intentionality of doing nothing. To become overwhelmed and frozen into inaction and lethargy is not good; but to decide to do nothing is bad.

But there's more to it than just that. From a purely selfish point of view, being lazy may be a totally rational decision. If you can get someone else to do the difficult things (tricky work, hard decisions, etc.) and still have a decent standard of

---

11 Around AD 600, Pope Gregory took the Eight Evil Thoughts of the fourth-century monks and rationalized them into the Seven Deadly Sins. In the course of that, acedia became sloth and lost some of its distinctive – and soul-corroding – attributes.

living, might you not make that choice? After all, doesn't it say in Ecclesiastes: "Everything is meaningless. What do people gain from all their labours at which they toil under the sun?... So I commend the enjoyment of life, because there is nothing better for a person under the sun than to eat and drink and be glad"[12] (1:2–3, 8:15 NIV)? Well, yes, it does say that, but that comes at a cost: your personal development may well be stunted, and you may well be massively undershooting your potential. But that's not all, because while the effects of laziness on the lazy person are important, we also need to look at the effects that that person has on those around them, and, particularly for our purposes, at the effect they have on their co-workers and on the workplace.

Laziness: the work doesn't get done

The most obvious effect of laziness in the workplace is on how the work there gets done, and by whom. If in an office of ten people, for example, one hundred tasks need performing every day, but one worker only does one of those tasks, then the other nine will have to do eleven. In addition to putting additional pressure on the nine, it is also dispiriting to see one of their number getting away with doing less. So, the consideration is not just the effect of more physical work (whether of hands or mind) for the nine, but also the effect on morale. Together, more work and less satisfaction will adversely impact the lives of others, and that, in turn, may seep into their family life, to relationships with their friends, and ultimately to their view of a just God ("Why, God? What are you thinking? Why do you let them get away with it?" – a theme of several psalms). And this touches back on the idea of Miroslav Volf we referred to earlier: that we are co-workers with God in His ongoing act

---

12 "Merry" in the King James Version.

of healing creation. If everyone is fed up and grumpy, and if things are not working as they are meant to, then God's work – and God's wish for us – is being harmed.

Or, to look at this from a slightly different angle, maybe the other nine don't each pick up the extra task. So, instead, the business now only performs ninety-one tasks each day. If those tasks (as I tend to assume) produce beneficial results for others, then the community (and broader creation) is a little less well off. And perhaps the business also does less well financially, so everyone gets paid a little less, and consequently can do a little less for their family or their favourite charity. Everyone and everything can be affected.

So far we've looked at what happens if one of our peers, roughly an equal, is lazy. But another different, although still relatively obvious, case is what can happen when our boss is lazy. I had a boss once (although not for very long) for whom nothing was too trivial to delegate, and for whom, following my completion of that task, nothing was too trivial to take credit for. I wondered – fruitlessly – how that boss managed to achieve a managerial position, but understood how they got to keep it (thanks to me, and others). This is not to say that many types of work don't require a hierarchy (they do), and that work often needs to be split up and/or delegated (it does).[13] But it is to say that a lazy boss can have negative effects that differ from those caused by a fellow worker, because there is more to it than simply the work of ten that now needs to be done by nine. What I and my fellow workers found with that boss was that it was totally dispiriting and demotivating to see someone who was meant to be a leader and setting a positive example, instead just freeloading. What's the example being

13 Although I'll still often agonize about whether to delegate something or not: am I delegating the work because a) it's boring, b) I'm lazy, c) my direct report needs the experience, d) my direct report can do it better than I can, e) my value-add comes in performing other tasks? And so on, and so on.

set there? Do just enough work until you get promoted into a position where you can pass all future work on to others? See how many people you can fool along the way? Show how much you really think of the place? The implicit (sometimes, explicit) promise of so many workplaces that if you "work hard, then you'll do well" begins to sound a little hollow. And with that boss cynicism quickly set in. A lazy boss can disastrously diminish the potential of the workplace – so, that's why I wriggled away from mine as soon as I could…

Laziness: disruption

There's another effect of our lazy colleague on the workplace, however, which, though less obvious, is just as – or perhaps even more – pernicious. And it's what Paul is getting at in the Scripture passage from his second letter to the Thessalonian Church (whom he'd had to leave in a hurry, and before he could get them properly sorted out). In this passage, he refers to those who are not only "idle" but also "disruptive". And these two are linked in two ways. First, extending the thought in the last paragraph, the idle may also be disruptive because they set an example that others might find attractive – or, at least, hard to resist. If the actions of the idle encourage a levelling down to the lowest common denominator, meaning that everyone works less, or everyone looks to someone else to carry the load to allow them to live the good life (and eat, drink, and be glad/merry), that will not only be idleness, but will, additionally, cause disruption. And, second, disruption may occur because – to use a very Victorian-sounding phrase to which I'll return – "the devil makes work for idle hands". In other words, the character trait which inspired the laziness may also inspire troublemaking. There are various interesting "chicken-and-egg" issues that we could pause on here,[14] but it is the effect on the workplace – on both the work and the other workers – which concerns us, and concerned Paul.

In my first job at the French bank, there was one notorious character who embodied this. Not just were they lazy, and more than content to let others do their work for them, but they then filled the time thus freed up by gossiping maliciously and telling grotesquely inappropriate jokes which deeply upset many of the women in the bank. Wherever they showed up, the mood curdled and the atmosphere turned slightly sour. So, our lazy colleague may end up negatively affecting the workplace, not just in a passive sense (they sit on their hands and the work does not get done), but also in an active sense through the disruption they cause. The rhythm (and potential) of the workplace can be disrupted both because they may encourage others to follow them, and because they have the time on their hands to cause mischief and create trouble.

Laziness: the myth of effortless ease

One final, slightly different form of laziness I want to look at is that caused by what we might call the myth of "effortless ease". This is a pervasive and persistent idea that manifests itself in many forms, whether you're an aspiring novelist/poet/artist, for example, or a fairly normal teenager – that it is somehow better, preferable, even commendable, to be successful without showing what hard work it was to get there. The phrase was often used in relation to British Edwardian gentlemen – those fortunate men upon whom the blessings of providence had been showered, and to whom good outcomes apparently

---

14 Does a tendency to laziness, for example, then leave time for troublemaking; or do troublemakers shirk work in order to make time for troublemaking? Does the "devil" seek out those with time on their hands; or do those with time on their hands seek out the devil?

came naturally, smoothly, and effortlessly. It encapsulated the idea that impressive results flowed from natural gifts (as became the gentleman's station in life) rather than anything so utilitarian as hard work and effort. For some teenagers today, the language would be slightly different – but, in much the same way, any success they have must absolutely not, in any way, be attributable to anything that could be associated with being a hard-working nerd.

I've criticized mindless hard work before, and will do again, but "effortless ease" really is a damaging idea, not because it wouldn't be wonderful if we could achieve great results with little effort, but because the practical outcomes of adopting this idea (myth) are often not great results, but very bad ones – bad both for our business and for us. How is that? Well, occasionally, and obviously, it simply gives the lazy an excuse to be lazy. But more insidious than that, it can lull some people into thinking that everything really should be easy. So, while they do want to succeed, they are made to believe that they will be able to do so with minimal effort because things will work out. But even beyond that, perhaps the most damaging aspect is that for some people it can break the link between the effort that goes into work, and the pleasure and rewards that flow from succeeding in that work. We are left feeling slightly guilty at all the hard work that was required to get the good result – if we were truly "chosen", wouldn't it have come with simply effortless ease? Therefore, we have somehow failed. Our pleasure in our work (which we do for and with God, remember) is thereby diminished, not because the outcome is bad, but because if we had been doing it "properly" it shouldn't have been so difficult. And, so, the pleasure we would otherwise get from hard work, the satisfaction of achievement through substantial effort, is diminished – thereby greatly lessening our incentive and desire to ever work hard.

Going back to the story of my undergraduate days, while there were both laziness and optimism at work here, as we'll discuss later, this idea of effortless ease also had a tight grip on us. Nobody wanted to be the nerd in the library studying for the highest grade. Instead we were enticed (and willingly fooled) by apocryphal stories of brilliant one-liners that secured the top grades (Essay question: "What is a joke?" Answer: "This is."), and stories of heroic drinking bouts through the night before the finals, followed by a brilliant, extempore paper in the exam room that carried all before it. The more prosaic, actual result, however, was that despite some of the most brilliant minds in the country being available to teach us, and almost limitless resources at our disposal, we instead felt the need to exhibit an air of nonchalance (laziness) that resulted in us wasting much of that opportunity.

Being the Good Samaritan: showing mercy

We've painted a fairly grim picture of the lazy colleague so far. And in the Bible passage for this chapter, Paul uses some harsh language about them and how the community should react to them (he didn't want the new Christians of Thessalonica to miss his point). So, we need to pause here for a moment and regroup – because this looks like one of those clear-cut (and God-given!) opportunities to righteously judge, condemn, and, finally, punish. And that plays to one of our greatest human weaknesses: the temptation to play God. Oh, come on, some of you will say. Paul is pretty clear about what to do – read them the Riot Act, shun them, deprive them of their unearned sustenance. Where's the nuance? And, anyway, some of you might continue, didn't you talk about the devil making work for idle hands? Isn't that a judgment, too?

Well, yes: Paul wrote what he wrote, and I wrote what I

wrote. And there is no doubt at all that some lazy people can be intensely annoying. But the subheading of this section refers to "showing mercy". So, we need to be careful about showing mercy only in the fashion of the Spanish Inquisition. Take the phrase I used about "idle hands". It contains an essential truth – but it should also be remembered that it was used by Victorian mill owners, and others, in a rapidly industrializing age to justify punishingly long hours and unfettered exploitation of child labour. And the use to which "work vs laziness" has been put in the twentieth-century work camps and gulags might give us pause (up to, and including, the ultimate perversion: *Arbeit Macht Frei/ Work Makes You Free*, above the gates at Auschwitz). No – while laziness is definitely a problem for the workplace, showing mercy requires something more imaginative than judgment and punishment.

Showing mercy: sharing our enthusiasm

Paul suggests part of a merciful answer in his letter. It's about setting an example, he says, and not allowing the disruption to spread. It's about being alongside the lazy colleague whether they're senior, junior, or at the same level, and showing by your conduct that work has value and gives life meaning. It's about setting an example for others by not standing on our own rights, whatever support – or exemptions – we ourselves may be due. But again, this makes it sound a little austere, possibly rather preachy, and slightly too instructional.

So, let me put it a little differently. We should try to show and to share some of the pleasure and fulfilment that we get out of a full work life. In this way, by encouraging and inspiring our lazy colleague to be otherwise (rather than by admonishing them or instructing them) we can truly show mercy. Part of this can be by simply letting people observe you work hard. But it should often be more proactive than that. If you have a job you love, tell people why. If there are some particularly fascinating aspects, communicate those. If there are stories that show how it's fun, share them with others. Show mercy through your commitment and enthusiasm.

Finally, pay attention to your lazy colleague. Laziness may take the form of inattention to detail, but it can also take the form of inattention to other people. Listen to your lazy colleague; be with them; really pay (and show that you are paying) attention to them. Again, it may light a spark, and inspire reciprocity.

Showing mercy: tackling "effortless ease"

A way of showing mercy in regard to effortless ease, which is perhaps a slightly separate facet of setting an example, described above, is to show that "working is cool". This sounds like a middle-aged parent trying to be young again, so I won't dwell too long on this aspect. But the point here is less about trying to encourage the lazy to work harder as we discussed in the last paragraph, and more about trying to encourage those perfectly willing to work that they shouldn't be discouraged because they don't match up to the false standard of effortless ease. So, think back to school, and the teacher who actually inspired you to work. They didn't do that by lecturing, or shouting, or droning on at you. They did it by making the subject interesting, relevant, often interactive, sometimes competitive, but almost always fun. They made you want to work; they made you see the point in working and what you could get out of it. There was no idea of languid, effortless ease – some things are hard and complicated – but the fun those teachers created was by enabling you to clearly see that what you got out was directly related to what you put in.

And that's what we need to recreate in the workplace: the idea that what we're doing is worthwhile, that it can be interesting, and that it is something where the more we put in the more we will get out. Not necessarily only in monetary rewards, but also in so many other ways which, in the end, will add up to true fulfilment.

Showing mercy: getting to the root

That said, I am not so naïve after thirty years in the workplace to believe that setting an example and/or sharing our passion is always going to be enough. But even when those don't work, showing mercy is not about us wielding the sharp-edged sword of justice. Laziness can be a real problem in the workplace – annoying, distracting, time-consuming – and one that truly needs to be dealt with. But that does not have to be done harshly if there is another way of doing it. And Paul hints at this also in his letter. Make them feel ashamed, he says, but do not treat them as an enemy – instead, warn them as a fellow believer. In other words, the purpose of the "naming and shaming" is to bring them back into the fold, rather than (simply) to punish them. And how is this to be done? By example, but also by a process that, to be sure, points out the problem, but which also leaves the door open. In the modern workplace, this should manifest itself in several ways – none of which involves us lecturing our colleague. There should be performance reviews that catch the issue before it becomes a serious problem. There should be feedback processes that allow colleagues to raise concerns, again before these begin to seriously impact the wider workplace. And, most importantly, there should be a protocol, including a performance plan which allows for improvement (redemption) rather than instant dismissal (judgment, punishment).

After all (it is really important to remember), the lazy colleague is a human being, never just an object or a "problem". And often they will be a human being in whom someone once saw some spark, some potential. What happened to that spark, that potential? Unless the colleague lied to get the job in the first place, what was it that went wrong? And can it now be righted? Did something happen at work that not just demotivated, but also embittered them? A traumatic experience with a boss; or being placed in a job to which they weren't suited but were then not allowed to transfer out of? Did something happen at home – a bitter divorce; the loss of someone very close – that was so shattering that they lost their bearings and began to lash out at an apparently heartless world? "Showing mercy", in this case, is HR and the boss of the lazy colleague working through these possibilities (and it can involve us, their colleague, as noted above, paying them attention and listening, showing that we do care). Not naively, and certainly naming the difficulty and trouble the laziness and disruptive trouble-making have caused for others. But, nevertheless, with the ultimate aim, with the ultimate hope, that a job can be salvaged – and, even more importantly, that a life can be turned around.

Being the injured man: accepting mercy

And, finally, back to us – you, me – lying in the road. If we're the lazy colleague, the obvious aspect of accepting mercy is to take the criticism, change our ways, and accept that we owe a fair day's work for a fair day's wages. But that is hardly revelatory, so, instead, I want to return again to the story with which I started.

Accepting mercy: laziness vs "busy-ness"

There is no doubt that my undergraduate friends and I did not work as hard as we could have done. And in so doing (or, rather *not* doing) we missed (or failed to fully take up) some of the remarkable, enormously privileged opportunities that had been placed in our laps. There was certainly some physical

– and perhaps also some mental – laziness. By contrast, at law school, no one could accuse my classmates who were pulling the all-nighters of physical laziness. But I subsequently wondered about the undiscriminating reading of every case from beginning to end, about the verbatim lecture notes, and about the long days and endless nights that exhausted so many. While certainly not laziness in the usual sense, might that attitude, in a sense that literalness, nevertheless add up to a lack of imagination that might be a form of mental laziness? A lack of imagination that says, for example, that something can only be done in a particular direct, head-on way, and can only be done with a certain brute force.

Why might this be a lack of imagination? Well, while it is true that as a lawyer you often need to work hard to assemble facts, to master the law, to understand the precedents – there can be no substitute, and no short cuts on the basics – you also need to be able to spot patterns and themes; to make new linkages; to have flashes of insight. And those may not come in a sleep-deprived state as you try to read everything ever written. Sometimes that revelation, that moment when everything slots into place, can only be achieved, or found, or discerned, by tiptoeing around the side of something, rather than by battering it head-on. By holding it up to the light at an unusual, unfamiliar angle. By stopping, and watching, and waiting for something new to emerge. And that is not just a question of hours expended; it is sometimes a question of actively stepping back, pausing, and waiting for something to happen.

Accepting mercy: laziness vs leisure

But there's even more to this mercy than stepping away from busy-ness and physically and mentally refreshing ourselves, ready to come back to work better and with more insight – important though that is to our role in the workplace as co-workers with God. There's also the damage that constant, unremitting busy-ness can do to us as human beings, as God's creatures.

I am now – my undergraduate days long behind me – something of an expert at stuffing my diary far too full of meetings and trips, and saying "yes" to tasks when I should long ago have started to say "no". In conventional terms, it would be hard to call me lazy, but a year or so ago, my spiritual director – who always has higher aspirations for me than mere busy-ness – suggested (insistently) that I read a short book by a post-war Catholic philosopher, Josef Pieper, called *Leisure: The Basis of Culture*.[15] I struggled, of course, to find the time. But when I eventually did, it was a remarkable read.

But before I get to Pieper, I want to pull together a couple of what may look like loose threads. I've just talked about being far too busy. I also talked a little earlier about the problem of "effortless ease" and pretending that work can be/should be/ is easy, when in fact it is hard. And even before that I talked about laziness as a positive choice to do nothing. That said, I don't, however, believe that the appropriate response to those who argue that it's all right to make a positive choice to do no work, is to argue instead that we should make a positive choice to work all the time. That choice to always be busy may itself be a lazy, default position. And, additionally, it is an unhelpful, "antagonistic opposite", if you will. What we need to find is, rather, something that is a "complementary opposite". Something else that is very different from work to be sure, something else, certainly, that prevents us from simply working all the time, but something else that also expands us as human beings – and quite possibly, but in no way necessarily, including when we are at work. That complementary opposite is, I believe, "leisure".

15 Josef Pieper, *Leisure: The Basis of Culture* (1963 edition, Ignatius Press 2009).

Josef Pieper and "leisure"

In very rough terms what Pieper says is that when our lives are only filled with "utilitarian" work – work done with the aim of earning money, or done with the aim of amassing material goods – then we will be less complete human beings, because the work feeds only our bodies, not our minds (souls). We also need "leisure" to be complete. (This is, he makes very clear, not the same as idleness/laziness.) Put slightly differently, in this other sphere we also need to be active, but in a way that is not "work". Traditionally, this is often thought of as contemplation (as in prayer, stillness, and quietness). But it might also be reading, or going to a play or concert, or looking at art – or, perhaps making clear to friends and colleagues that we have the time to welcome "idle" conversation with them, have time to really listen, have time just to be with another person. It is any activity which takes us beyond ourselves and the present moment; which leads us to appreciate that there is something bigger (and better) than ourselves.

For the "busy" person in a pressured job this may sound difficult – not everyone has a handy cloister to visit. But it is not impossible: there is art on the internet; music on your phone; and poetry (and the Bible) in thin, small, pocket-size volumes, all of which can be looked at/listened to/read during a break in the day. And we can also make ourselves available to our colleagues at work, as much as to our friends outside – even over coffee in the staff canteen, or walking out for a sandwich at lunchtime. And, of course, none of this is really new. St Benedict who founded the order of Benedictine monks, in his "Rule" for how the monks should live, envisaged a life that mixed physical work with communal meals, contemplation, and worship. It's a sense of perspective that it's really easy to lose – but incredibly valuable to regain.

But it is also very important that this not become about doing these things in order to be able to check them off a list. Pieper's insight is that doing these things precisely because they are not "utilitarian" is what broadens our perspective and feeds our soul. And it is this – alongside work to put food on the table and a roof over our head – that makes for a fuller and more complete life.

Accepting mercy: Sabbath moments

I occasionally think of these short periods of leisure as "Sabbath moments" – times when we can refresh ourselves by letting the Spirit take us where it will. I'm not particularly lyrical, but let me give one slightly extended example of something that lifted my soul. In a recent October, I drove 1,000 miles in four days, criss-crossing New England. At dawn on one of those days, on my way to yet another meeting, I drove through the Green Mountains in Vermont. For many miles, mine was the only car on the road. The rising sun touched first the mountaintops, and then cut into the steep, dark valleys. The leaves were changing, with splashes of yellows, reds, and golds across the hills, outlined against an intense blue sky. And once, as I stopped to marvel at an almost infinite view, I caught the faint smell of woodsmoke on the air. Decades of memories swept over me, powerful and poignant; but also a profound anticipation of a less frenetic future where I could pause more often to wonder at the simple, complex beauty of God's creation.

And for that hour, I ceased to worry about US and UK politics, and cost-cutting at work, and the overdue-but-unwritten memo, and the unpopularity of big business, and my next meeting, and corporate tax, and all the other things that regularly whirl through my mind throughout my day. For that moment (that hour), even as my body moved, my mind stopped, drank deeply, and I felt at peace. In that moment,

the intensity made up for any brevity. I was doing nothing…
and yet I was open to so many possibilities in what was truly a
moment of grace.

It won't always be a mountain range; as I've already said, it
may be a painting, or some music, or the way the sunlight falls,
or the wind blows, or the clouds move across the sky. But these
Sabbath moments of leisure – not laziness – can suddenly
take us out of ourselves, out of the busy-ness of our lives, can
still our minds, and can refresh our souls. To allow these to
happen, to recognize their value, to welcome them, is truly to
accept mercy.

So, those college afternoons spent reading novels, talking
politics, or even cooking, were, perhaps, not all time wasted.
Possibly some of that was creative "leisure" – time for our
soul; time for others. And, by the same token, the incredibly
long hours of some of my law school classmates were maybe
too "utilitarian", too focused on the sole end of acquiring a
practical skill. To be sure, studying for a university degree
is different from working for a salary. Expectations are very
different – but Pieper's insight still applies. Many of us have
been taught, conditioned, to believe that more time spent
working is good, and less time spent working is bad. But we
will be fuller human beings – and our workplace will benefit
– if we can balance our lives, not with something vs nothing,
but with something vs something else. Work and leisure. And
that requires of you two things: courage and imagination. The
courage to find time in your working life for something that
doesn't sound like work to many people. And the imagination
to understand that some leisure, rather than constant busy-
ness, is the true opposite of laziness.

6

THE VERBOSE COLLEAGUE

Pursue love and strive for the spiritual gifts, and especially that you may prophesy. For those who speak in a tongue do not speak to other people but to God; for nobody understands them, since they are speaking mysteries in the Spirit. On the other hand, those who prophesy speak to other people for their upbuilding and encouragement and consolation. Those who speak in a tongue build up themselves, but those who prophesy build up the church. Now I would like all of you to speak in tongues, but even more to prophesy. One who prophesies is greater than one who speaks in tongues, unless someone interprets, so that the church may be built up. Now, brothers and sisters, if I come to you speaking in tongues, how will I benefit you unless I speak to you in some revelation or knowledge or prophecy or teaching? It is the same way with lifeless instruments that produce sound, such as the flute or the harp. If they do not give distinct notes, how will anyone know what is being played? And if the bugle gives an indistinct sound, who will get ready for battle?

So with yourselves; if in a tongue you utter speech that is not intelligible, how will anyone know what is being said? For you will be speaking into the air. There are doubtless many different kinds of sounds in the world, and nothing is without sound. If then I do not know the meaning of a sound, I will be a foreigner to the speaker and the speaker a foreigner to me. So with yourselves; since you are eager for spiritual gifts, strive to excel in them for building up the church. Therefore, one who speaks in a tongue should pray for the power to interpret.

1 Corinthians 14:1–13 NRSV

One Sunday evening I arrived at the airport unusually early for a flight, with the optimistic plan of clearing some of my ever-growing backlog of emails. Seated opposite me were a middle-aged man and his sprightly, if elderly, mother. Almost as soon as I sat down and opened my computer, however, the man's phone rang. It was his nephew, who would, I soon learned, turn sixteen the following day. In increasingly (to me) agonizing detail, the man explained three times, in almost identical terms, why he and his mother would not be there for the birthday, how they planned to visit later in the month, when the nephew's present would arrive, why it had been delayed, and on and on and on and on. Three times! Having squeezed the last drop of juice from this completely banal conversational lemon, he then ran through the same process with what the boy was doing at school. Again, with both painful detail and extravagant repetition, he flogged this new, equally inconsequential topic as hard as he could, and from every conceivable angle, until it, too, losing the will to live, collapsed under the weight of the man's torrent of words and died. With a host of uncharitable thoughts racing through my mind (and completely distracted from my unread emails) I waited in horror to see what he would move on to next. It was at that point that I saw – with glee I suspect I barely disguised – his mother impatiently gesture for the phone. He reluctantly handed it over. "As your uncle just told to you," she started, "we can't make it for your birthday tomorrow because…"

Verbosity: two frightening phrases

When I sit in meetings there are two sets of phrases that always make me slump back in my chair. The first starts with something like: "At the risk of repeating what has already been said…", or "I hate to repeat myself, but…", or "Just to re-emphasize the point again…", or "To restate that in a slightly different way…" What this first set all add up to, regardless of the slight variation in language, is a warning that – despite the fervent protestations of not wishing to – the person is indeed intent on repeating what has already been said (and often more than once). The second set of phrases always starts something like this: "I know I only have five minutes, but it might be worth getting into a little more detail…", or "The details are worth pausing on for just a moment…", or "I do have a few/several/ fifty slides which contain more detail than I will speak to, but just to look at a few details for a moment…" Again, as with the first set of phrases, the key is the protestation of brevity, which is transparently untrue (or, to be slightly more charitable, physically impossible, given the nature of the detail).

Now, of course, there are occasions when repetition can serve a purpose – if a difficult concept is being explained for the first time, for example, or if the language of the meeting is not the first language of everyone attending. But, more often, repetition arises because, for example, people come prepared to speak about something and then don't want to sit silently before their boss, or an external audience, and say nothing simply because the person who spoke before them just said what they were planning to say. Or it arises because people feel they can say it better than it has been said before (even if only incrementally). Or because some people – although, thankfully, only a small number in almost all the meetings I go to – like the sound of their own voice. Now to be very clear, while these phrases do fill me with dread, I, inevitably, have also inflicted them on others at certain points in my career – and in the case of the very last (liking the sound of my own voice), may do so still.

Verbosity: repetition

But what's wrong with that, you ask? Other than being slightly boring, is there anything truly negative about repetition? Is there anything really wrong with details? Well, I think there are a couple of answers to that. The first is that there is truth to the maxim that time wasted never returns. Time spent – wasted – engaging in repetition, is time that cannot be spent on something else. That may not be significant if the time would otherwise have been spent staring out of the window or surfing the web. But if it prevents other work from being done that could have helped our business (or helped our co-workers) then that is a loss. Likewise, if it means we have to stay later or longer at work to get the job done, instead of spending time at home with family or friends, that is also a loss. And, remembering what we said in the last chapter, if it removes time for leisure – or induces such frustration as to make that leisure impossible – then that, too, is a loss. To be clear, repetition can squander business resources, no less than overly generous business lunches, or the latest vanity overhaul of the corporate logo.

Closely related to this is the fact that time spent engaged in repetition or excessive detail on one topic may squeeze out the time needed to discuss another topic of importance. Often, in many settings, the time for meetings or phone calls is limited. So, if repetition on the first topic spins out of control, then time for discussion of the second topic may get squeezed. It may be possible to reschedule, but it may also be that the second topic simply never gets the time it needs – again to the disadvantage of the business and those working on that second topic.

But beyond the issue of the direct impact on the work of the business, there is the equally (or, perhaps, more) important effect on people in the business. Some people do indeed have the patience of a saint, but most people (which definitely includes me) do not. So, the boredom and frustration engendered by meandering meetings, or convoluted conference calls, or extravagantly detailed conversations, that are engendered by the inability of someone to control themselves and/or by the inability of others to control them – all of these impact our work. Whether it is annoyance at our colleague, or at our ineffective boss; whether the principal emotion is, indeed, frustration and anger, or boredom and demotivation, doesn't really matter. Less inspired by our work and workplace, we will put less effort into it, and while that obviously impacts the business for which we work, it also impacts us personally as we stretch ourselves less, drifting further away from a full realization of what we could be.

Moving on a little from boredom, there is also the corrosive impact that the encouragement or, at least, toleration, of verbosity – whether repetition, or unnecessary detail – might have. If succinctness is neither valued nor rewarded, then our thinking may become sloppier. President Woodrow Wilson, when asked how long it took him to prepare a speech, is reputed to have said: "It depends. If I am to speak ten minutes,

I need a week for preparation; if fifteen minutes, three days; if half an hour, two days; if an hour, I am ready now."[16] It does take effort and discipline to refine and reduce an argument without losing its essence – rambling around it may be much easier, but considerably less rigorous.

Another related aspect is where everyone is encouraged in – or no one is prevented from – saying pretty much the same thing in their own, ever-so-slightly different way. Whether it's to catch the boss's eye, or listen to one's own voice, it can encourage one-upmanship and increasingly baroque attempts to cloak the concept already mentioned (several times) in ever more extravagant detail, and at ever greater length. Nothing is achieved – other than, perhaps, the dangerous delusion that quantity = quality. While I am not, generally, a huge fan of this phrase (which is used, for example, to excuse many varieties of cost-cutting): less in this case really can be more.

Verbosity: extravagant detail

Moving on to verbosity in relation to detail rather than repetition, there is, first, a pernicious possibility that needs to be considered. Namely, that verbosity becomes an intentional business strategy, for example, in sectors such as advisory and consultancy services. In a world where value often equates to time spent, there will be incentives to expend as much time as possible on a project. If, for example, at a law firm you are given a 2,200-hour annual target, and especially if work is a little hard to come by, lengthy meetings to explore – exhaustively – every single, possible avenue might hold a certain (commercial) attraction. And this exhaustiveness can become part of the

---

16 The attribution is probably correct, but there are plenty of variants on it attributed to others. In a similar vein, Churchill (along with Blaise Pascal, Mark Twain, and others) is reputed to have once said: "I apologize for writing you a long letter, but I did not have time to write you a short one."

culture, so that even when there is plenty to be done, the only acceptable way of doing things is (over-) comprehensively and meticulously, regardless of the needs of the client, or the justifiable allocation of resources to that project. There was a standing joke in the US firms that I worked for about the mythical (although devoutly-to-be-desired) "Fifty-State Survey", where a foolish, imprecise, or novice client didn't frame their enquiry tightly enough and ended up with an exhaustive review of the impact of a certain transaction in every single state of the union. Not strictly necessary, perhaps; not the most productive use of the brains involved, perhaps; but most definitely very lucrative. Blessed are the verbose…

Another slightly less malign, but nevertheless still detrimental, effect that a focus on excessive detail can lead to is a lack of strategic vision for the business with significant long-term (and occasionally short-term) impacts. Setting strategic direction requires getting above the details sometimes, looking for trends and thinking intuitively. If, however, we are always "down in the weeds", only ever focused on detail – whether the exact placement of goods on the shelves of a supermarket, or the minutiae of legal rules affecting a transaction – we may miss other questions that go to the essence of a business: what are the trends of the future, where is the market going? (Not to mention: should we be going in this direction; and what might God want in this?) Details and tactics are important, and should never be neglected. But nor should the big picture. And while verbosity certainly also exists in some strategic discussions (which can be fertile ground for ever-changing jargon, and expansive geopolitical clichés), getting tangled in the details can definitely detract from strategic thinking.

Verbosity: speaking to be understood

Which brings us (after what some might identify as a leisurely stroll through the potential problems caused by verbosity that is itself, well, slightly verbose...) to the passage from Paul's letter to the Corinthians. Speaking in tongues is something that tends to alarm the middle-of-the road Christian, to the point that most of the Bible passages relating to it are simply avoided by many churches/preachers/readers. Which is a shame. Tongues, while they may not be your cup of tea, are a vital manifestation of the Holy Spirit at work in the world. The Spirit grabs each of us in different ways if we let it, and we should no more look down on speaking in tongues than we would the Spirit driving us into an unexpected act of generosity, or into rapture over a piece of art or music. So, it's important to note that Paul is not saying that speaking in tongues is bad (he spoke in them), any more than I am saying that speaking at length is bad (and I'll come to that later). What he is saying, however, is that there is a time and place for speaking in tongues, and a time and place for speaking comprehensibly. While we might, by speaking in tongues, want to show our joy at the inspiration of the Spirit, or at the wonder of our faith, we need to remember that our most important job is building up the church and spreading the gospel to those who have not yet heard it. And so, by analogy, for me the message of this passage for life in the office is that while detail is important, and may reflect both the passion we have for our job and the time we have devoted to learning its every in and out, to go on and on about it may not always be the best for our business, or for our colleagues, or for God's work there. We must consider our audience, what we are trying to achieve, and be careful not to alienate or exclude them.

As part of my job, I run a small group that sponsors economic research from leading academics into business tax issues. Over the years it has done some really interesting work, and the research papers are (I am assured by others!) very highly thought of. The papers themselves are often 30–40 pages long, and filled with tables of extensive regression analyses and lengthy equations with lots of Greek characters. However, our charitable purpose is to educate the public at a conference once a year. So, our research director, who is a very distinguished and senior academic economist, spends hours with the researchers on the presentations that will be made at the conference. Tables are turned into simple graphs; equations are turned into prose. And the researchers are reminded again, and again: "Your aim is to communicate a message; not to show how much you know." The research director and I know how good the researchers are – and tell them frequently – but the purpose of the meeting is to communicate and inform; not overwhelm and exclude.

Paul writes: "if in a tongue you utter speech that is not intelligible, how will anyone know what is being said? ... I will be a foreigner to the speaker and the speaker a foreigner to me." That is the danger of verbosity – whether repetition, or detail – that we become "a foreigner to the speaker, and the speaker a foreigner to me." So, however passionate we feel, we should judge our audience and our purpose according to their needs and abilities, rather than ours. And having done that we should then try to speak as succinctly, and with such level of detail (but no more), as will build up our colleagues and our business – both of which God cares about – rather than diminish them.

Being the Good Samaritan: showing mercy

What does showing mercy to our verbose colleague involve? I think it is important to make two things clear at the start. First, mercy has to be involvement and engagement rather than disengagement. However annoying our colleague's verbosity might be, we should try not to walk away, or yawn, or snigger behind our hands. And second, whatever our frustration, that engagement must be thoughtful and generous, rather than mean-spirited and judgmental. To return to the theme of Paul's letter for a moment, we shouldn't disparage verbosity (either detail or repetition), but, when appropriate, we should point out how it may disadvantage our other colleagues as individuals, as well as the business as a whole. And we should also point out to our colleague the personal benefits to them that may flow from not always feeling the need to speak at length (especially if they are only echoing what has already been said), or dive into subterranean detail at the first opportunity.

Showing mercy: running meetings (part 2)

So, when you are running a meeting, one way of showing mercy to your verbose colleague (and others) is to make clear at the beginning that you will hold people to time, you will get through the agenda, and that everyone will get to contribute something. Signalling that in advance (and perhaps even privately before that) will give your verbose colleague time to prepare – will give them the time to compose Wilson's short speech or Churchill's short letter. It is absolutely not about humiliation during the meeting. It is about showing all of the people involved in the meeting that you care about them – all of them, and the business – enough, that you are prepared to be firm in order to ensure that everyone is heard and everything is discussed. I inherited one of my committee chair roles with a tradition of open-ended meetings with relatively high-level agendas that terminated late in the afternoon as people drifted off to catch weekend trains. And across those wide-open spaces of that slightly unfocused agenda, conversations expanded to fill the hours, meandering gently across the open prairie that was the entire afternoon… and driving me to distraction. The other committee members were generally older, more experienced, and much more distinguished than I was, so I started off uncertain what to do. But the disadvantages were too clear to ignore, so we shifted the meetings to the morning with a hard start and a hard finish; we drew up more detailed agendas; I prepped some speakers. And, ever so gently, I cut others off as they began to circle back on themselves. We ended up getting more done in less time, hearing from more people, and with clearer decisions than before – and if some people felt offended, they could never quite bring themselves to tell me!

A slightly different context arises when not you but your boss is running the meeting. Then, perhaps, you go and speak to them, and in addition to making the points in the last paragraph about building up both people and the business by keeping to time and covering all subjects, you could make more specific points relating to your boss's role. You could describe how, when the boss is present, people often repeat what others have said because they fear if they do not speak they will be thought "shy", or "not team players", or even "weak". You can explain the common confusion – which can be exacerbated by some of the business productivity measurement tools ("metrics") – about the relative merits of quantity and quality. And you can explain the one-upmanship that can be involved when speaking in front of the boss. All of these your boss can address by making clear that speaking-up is not the only criterion employed in measuring job performance – or even the most important; that repetition is actually a negative rather than a positive; that excessive detail helps no one; and that one-upmanship will be duly (but unfavourably) noted.

But to a certain extent, rigorous timekeeping and traffic-directing only address a symptom rather than a cause. And mercy may involve getting to the root cause. There might be several aspects to this. First, in the same way that detail can be taught, so can succinctness. Both require training, application, and time. Time to order your thoughts, training to speak (and write) clearly and simply, and training to speak within allotted time limits. Another, slightly different element is training (or at least encouraging) people to be sensitive to those around them, to think what their verbosity might do to their colleagues and to the workplace as a whole. And still another element might be trying to discern whether there is something in someone's past experience that led to the verbosity: criticism for non-participation from an earlier boss; missing out on a promotion through lack of self-advertisement; being criticized for not fully explaining something which subsequently turned out to be highly relevant. In this last case neither you, nor your boss, alone may be able to find this out. But in conjunction with HR this may be worth exploring – because a person needs help, and a life may be improved.

Now, I am aware that all of these can require a certain steeliness that may not come naturally (most people don't get much pleasure out of being "cruel to be kind"), but the benefits to your colleague, your business, and you, can be very real, and genuinely merciful. As importantly, however, it requires a real commitment to other people and to the business. It's too easy to switch off as your colleague drones on, to accept it as an unavoidable cost, and surreptitiously go back to reading something more interesting on your laptop/iPad/iPhone. But what God wants, both for the verbose colleague (and for the business), is for you to get in there and try to do something about it – to be the neighbour to that colleague.

Being the injured man: accepting mercy

I have already voiced the suspicion that, upon occasion, others find me verbose. And, thus, I should take to heart the mercy shown by those who offer to me what I have suggested above. But, as you will also have realized, I feel quite strongly about the harm that can arise from repetition and dwelling upon unnecessary detail. And this, almost certainly, makes me too dismissive of both, even when there is a place for them. So, my real injury may be that dismissiveness; and true mercy – what my verbose colleague may give me – will lie in showing me the benefit of taking more time. Not categorizing everything that bores or frustrates me as worthless – but as something whose potential may be quite the opposite. I think there are three aspects to this: one slightly trite, a second, obvious but quite important, and a third, slightly less obvious, but even more important.

The slightly trite point is that patience genuinely is a virtue, while impatience genuinely is not. Sometimes, in fact, my impatience is really a kind of laziness; an unwillingness to take the time to pay attention to others. In our increasingly frantic world, patience (again, like leisure) can beneficially slow us down a bit. It can prick the illusion that we are always in control. It can suggest that there are some rhythms that we should not seek to speed up. It can remind us that people are more important than things (including targets and metrics). To be sure, excessive caution, the unwillingness to spend the time to write the short speech, or any of the other things that we have talked about above are not virtues either... but two wrongs don't make a right. Exercising the patience to hear someone out at length may sometimes be painful, but also good for us as individuals.

The second, obvious, but also quite important point is that excessive speed can prevent us from taking the time to recognize important aspects of an issue; and being too "succinct" can simply produce shallow thinking and sound bites, rather than sharper and more efficient outcomes. If the benefit in the preceding paragraph was personal, then the benefit here is more for the community (business, or other group). Because some things really do need time, really need considered reflection, really need to percolate through our brains, really need time to reach maturity. The headmaster at my kids' school often used to tell the students: "There's nothing wrong with going around the roundabout (gyratory) a second time." In other words, take your time to reach the right conclusion, rather than rushing immediately to a decision. It is mercy to be reminded of that.

The third, and slightly less obvious – but very valuable – point is that allowing some discussions to play out for longer than I might personally wish can benefit the team. I am certainly not talking about indulging people who truly do love the sound of their own voice, but I am talking about showing respect for those whose decision-making processes are different from mine. This is independent of whether the answer they get from going around the roundabout several times is better/worse/ different from the one I might arrive at on my first go-around. The point is that in a team we need to accommodate different ways of arriving at decisions, different ways of working, in order to nurture the team rather than just the individual. Speed and efficiency are important – but they are not everything. Even if I were always right (which I definitely am not) there can still be a real advantage to not always short-cutting things once the answer seems clear. The dynamics of the team and the business, and how it operates tomorrow, and the day after, and next week, can sometimes be more important than saving minutes, or even hours today. The process – and life – is often about more than simply getting to the quickest answer.

During my annual assessment in the final year of ordination training, my tutor, having said all the predictably nice things (I was just about to get ordained, so it was probably not the time to discourage me), nevertheless ended with a "but…" "But," he said, "smart though you undoubtedly are, and quick, too, your fellow students feel sometimes you come to conclusions too quickly, don't give them the time, don't hear them out. And that upsets them." That stopped me dead. For one used to moving forward – being expected to move forward in business – at full throttle, it was like being told that I'd been shoving other cars off the road and into the ditch without even noticing. In my year group, while I had been to university, some had not formally completed high school; and while I had been making decisions under pressure for over twenty years, others were retired, or in very different types of jobs. And I just didn't take account of that. I would sit there impatiently as people seemed to go on and on. I was happy to finish their sentences. I was happy, as soon as I could, to give what I regarded as the obvious answer to the easy question. But I realized then when my tutor told me (although I continue to forget it, again and again, and need reminding constantly), that regardless of whether I was right or wrong, the other students needed to know that I cared enough about them, and enough about the common journey that we were on, to take the time to listen to them, to pay attention to them, to actually respect them. To be a neighbour to them, so that they could be a neighbour to me.

And to be told that was mercy then, and, whenever I recall it, it is mercy now.

7

THE LONER

For just as the body is one and has many
members, and all the members of the body,
though many, are one body, so it is with Christ.
For in the one Spirit we were all baptized into
one body – Jews or Greeks, slaves or free –
and we were all made to drink of one Spirit.
Indeed, the body does not consist of one
member but of many. If the foot would say,
"Because I am not a hand, I do not belong
to the body," that would not make it any less
a part of the body. And if the ear would say,
"Because I am not an eye, I do not belong to
the body," that would not make it any less a
part of the body. If the whole body were an
eye, where would the hearing be? If the whole
body were hearing, where would the sense
of smell be? But as it is, God arranged the
members in the body, each one of them, as
he chose. If all were a single member, where
would the body be? As it is, there are many
members, yet one body. The eye cannot say to
the hand, "I have no need of you," nor again
the head to the feet, "I have no need of you."

On the contrary, the members of the body that seem to be weaker are indispensable, and those members of the body that we think less honourable we clothe with greater honour, and our less respectable members are treated with greater respect; whereas our more respectable members do not need this. But God has so arranged the body, giving the greater honour to the inferior member, that there may be no dissension within the body, but the members may have the same care for one another. If one member suffers, all suffer together with it; if one member is honoured, all rejoice together with it.

1 Corinthians 12:12–26 NRSV

The titles of all the other chapters in this section focus on the adjective before the word "colleague" – "ambitious", "shy", "verbose", and so on – to explore different types of our co-workers. Except for this one. "The Loner Colleague" doesn't sound quite right; in fact, "loner" seems more noun than adjective. The word might certainly include elements of "shy" and "ambitious" and "depressed", for example. But we all know the loner in the office, and none of those words alone quite captures it. We can try others. "Aloof", perhaps. "Strong", sometimes. "Unfriendly", occasionally. "Individualistic", politely. "Self-absorbed", less politely. "Anti-social", rudely. But "self-contained", always. We can also turn to popular phrases to try to capture it: "They plough their own furrow"; "march to the beat of their own drum". And, again, less politely: "don't play well in the sand-pit/box". What, I think, it often comes down to, however, is that the loner often just doesn't really feel like a colleague. "Colleague" carries connotations of cooperation –

however fractious and frustrating the individual may be – but the loner feels different. Less someone with whom you share a common purpose; more like a stranger on a train, who just so happens to be sitting next to you.

But, you might ask, in a corporate culture that so often seems to value conformity (despite the apparent paradox of a broader culture that elevates individual over community), what's wrong with "ploughing your own furrow" and trying to stand out from the crowd? What's wrong with that – particularly, if you can avoid the traps associated with ambition, such as wielding sharp elbows, and trampling others down? My answer to all that is: "nothing". However, at the same time, that's not exactly what I'm focusing on.

You can be a unique individual in a team; you can be a strong person in a team. But if you're a loner, then you're simply not really a member of the team in the first place. To use an obvious sporting analogy, if the striker on a football (soccer) team, however gifted they may be, doesn't cooperate with other members of the team (marking, passing the ball, thinking of themselves in relation to others) then the team will not play as well. Perhaps the striker is just so good at scoring goals that the team always wins – but the eleven will not function as a "team", and their full potential (as individuals and a unit) will not be reached. But if they did play as a true team, perhaps they could score even more goals together; perhaps each one of them might feel more fulfilled. So, the bare score, the bare number, is not quite the point. It's what that score, that number, could have been if the full potential had been realized by the team, rather than by the skill (brilliance, genius) of the loner. As we've seen before, allowing each person as an individual to fully develop their talents and to build and deepen relationships within the framework of a team, is what best promotes the human flourishing that God desires in the workplace (and everywhere). And the loner can severely disrupt that dynamic – just like Paul's unruly limbs.

Impact on the business and the team

So, to focus back on the workplace, what might be the problematic impacts of the loner? Well, I think they fall into at least three categories – each of which may vary slightly according to the type of workplace. One is the impact on the loner themselves, the second is the impact on the business, and the third is that on the loner's fellow workers. We'll look at the first in a moment, but the impacts of the second and third, in any line of business, are similar to the effects on that football/soccer team. Take the incredibly gifted salesperson who can talk anybody into anything. They may sell more than anyone else on the team, they may seem to boost the bottom line, they may be praised for their contribution... but something is missing. What if they shared some of their skill, some of their know-how with other team members? What if they took another team member on sales trips with them – might not the two of them sell more together than the superstar and the disheartened underling would ever do apart? What if the superstar loner took time to encourage, to teach, to inspire the other members of the team – might not everybody feel better, slightly more alive, closer to realizing their full potential? But the loner doesn't do that.

Or what about the superstar lawyer, a subject that I've touched on before? In a law firm partnership, the loner lawyer may be brilliant, may get great results for individual clients, may even enhance the reputation of the whole firm... but in my experience the partnership will rarely be stronger or better for their presence. The clue is in the name: partnership. If there are too many loners the partnership will operate less as a team or a community, and more like a collection of individuals sharing a workspace. The loner rarely takes others under their wing to train them, or to inspire them (other than acquiring the occasional protégé necessary for doing drafting and research). And the atmosphere is worsened rather than improved by having someone – however good – who clearly doesn't pay any attention to (far less care for) those around them either as colleagues or as human beings.

But it's also worth saying at this point that it's not exactly "selfishness" that we're talking about either – even if that's a term that often gets applied to loners. You can have a very selfish team member who uses the team to further their own ends – but the loner is different. Not misusing the team, so much as ignoring it. The loner is not really the cuckoo in the nest, living off the efforts of others; the loner is more the bird that builds a separate nest in the same tree and pays no attention whatsoever to any of the others. Nor is the loner opposed to the concept (or reality) of the team in the office – they simply don't want to be any part of it.

So, in a culture that at least pays lip service to teamwork, how – or why – do they survive? Well, the simple answer is that loners are usually rather good at what they do. In a sense that's obvious – if they weren't, they'd have been thrown out long ago. It is only because they bring some other significant benefit to the business that they are allowed to remain. This is in contrast to the incompetent and lazy colleagues, at whom we've already looked. Those two types detract from the potential of the office because of what they do, or don't do. But, almost by definition, the incompetent and lazy can only exist in an environment where a team makes up for their failings, covers for them, picks up the slack. That's not the case with the loner. The loner adversely affects the team, not because the loner imposes upon them, but, rather, because the loner has no need for them and, instead, totally ignores them.

It is that ignoring of business and colleagues – in Paul's terms, refusing to acknowledge that it is part of the body at all – where the problem lies. Paul has a number of targets in mind when he writes to the Corinthians, but one of them is to emphasize that they have been brought together in a common enterprise (body/church) by a common calling (baptism). They have left behind their history as people unconnected with one another, and defined by ancestry and status (Greeks, Jews, slaves, etc.) and have come together into a single unit with a common mind and purpose (the Spirit). But the body will not work if the parts do not acknowledge that they are, in fact, pieces of a single whole. The parallels with a workplace containing one or more loners are pretty clear: the loner ignores what has brought the enterprise together – the common purpose; ignores what keeps it together – the common calling; and ignores what it needs to be successful in the future – cooperation and mutual reliance. And that matters, because in the same way that the church enables us to be (beneficially) in relationship with other people, so do corporations, and companies, and partnerships (the etymology of each reflects a coming together). Any of these associations form, as we've seen before, another "neighbourhood". And it is this, at least in the medium and long term, that the loner damages and diminishes – the body that is the business; and the body that is his team of colleagues, his neighbours.

Impact on the loner

So, to the last effect the loner has – that on themselves. To think more about this, it's helpful to look at what it is that makes the loner tick. Again, the adjectives pile up – confidence, self-belief, arrogance maybe – but what it really seems to come down to is certainty that they can do everything themselves, that they have no need for others (sometimes including God). Now, there's something attractive about this when it manifests itself as a gutsy determination not to be dragged down by blind fate or by the limitation of others. But, at a certain point, that strength becomes a weakness that negatively impacts the loner themselves. That is the weakness that comes when self-sufficiency spills over into isolation. The weakness that comes when we are not simply in charge of our own lives, but also totally alone in them. The weakness that comes when we're isolated from others, and isolated from God. The weakness that comes when we're alone in life without a map, or reference points, or a compass. It is what happens when, as Paul writes, the eye tries to say to the hand, or the head to the feet, "I have no need of you." At its worst, the loner loses those necessary relationships with others and with God that make us fuller, more complete human beings. And when that point is reached, something has gone badly wrong.

Being the Good Samaritan: showing mercy

There's a powerful strain of nineteenth-century thought that celebrates what was then called "self-reliance". You can find it in the philosophical writings of Emerson, in novels, and in poems such as Kipling's "If" – beloved of generations of certain types of schoolmasters and, occasionally, pupils. But a prime example that still gets widely quoted today (in part, because of its connection with a recent movie) is by a Victorian poet called William Ernest Henley.

Henley had tuberculosis in the bones of his leg. In the 1870s the disease was incurable, and, while still a teenager, he had to have one leg amputated. In his early twenties, the other leg became infected, but, against his doctors' recommendations, he fought a second amputation. As he lay in hospital, facing huge odds, with no rational explanation for what had befallen him, he willed himself to succeed – in part by writing a poem, "Invictus", which ends with these well-known lines:

> It matters not how strait the gate,
> How charged with punishments the scroll.
> I am the master of my fate:
> I am the captain of my soul.

Almost a century later, Nelson Mandela, inspired by Henley's determination to struggle against the odds, quoted the same lines to himself and his fellow prisoners on Robben Island. He was determined that almost thirty years in jail, intended to break him physically and mentally, would do neither. He, too, succeeded.[17]

Showing mercy: examining self-reliance

And this is the attractive side of "self-reliance": it's standing firm when others run; it's keeping your head when all around you are losing theirs; it's being the master of your fate and captain of your soul. In the face of great, sometimes overwhelming odds, you keep on battling. When all seems lost, you keep on hoping and fighting. You don't listen to the naysayers, to the doubters, but you follow your convictions. You keep your eye on the Pole Star, and you know where north is on the compass. In slightly more prosaic business terms: you have faith in the plan when no one else does; you know to buy when others are selling; you have the vision for growth in new markets that no one else can see. You have the grit and determination to work, and work, and work when no one else does. And all of this is admirable – it genuinely is. There really are lonely heroes,

---

17 *Invictus* – from the title of Henley's poem – is a 2009 movie that tells the story of Nelson Mandela and the 1995 Rugby World Cup in South Africa.

and they really do make a difference. Whether it's Winston Churchill or Steve Jobs, the world would be different and slightly diminished without them. But when it's not just a case of standing out from the crowd, but also of standing away from it, there can start to be a cost. There's a tangible difference between the courage and hope that come from deep belief, and the overconfidence and hubris that come from thinking that we have all the answers and that we're self-sufficient. Put slightly differently, there's an enormous difference between thinking we've done it all ourselves, and acknowledging that we could only have done it with others (especially, God).

Showing mercy: aligning but not integrating

So how can we show mercy to the loner in the office? Well, I think it's important to say right at the beginning that it would *not* be showing mercy if we were to try to turn the loner into a fully paid-up team member. There is something fundamental in the character of a loner that means that both you and they would only experience pain, frustration, and failure as you tried to force a square peg into a round hole. It won't – it can't – happen. But mercy is most certainly possible if we try to work with, rather than against, the grain of their character. If we can do this, then at least two good things may happen. First, the rest of the office, the work community, the business, will truly benefit from their gifts. But, even more importantly, for the loner – even without having to join the team – it may lessen their isolation from others; an isolation which they have sought to ignore, or, perhaps, never even really knew existed.

So how do we do this? Well, perhaps a personal story might help. Many years ago, at one of the law firms at which I worked, I had a colleague who could be politely described as a loner – and about whom many of the more judgmental adjectives with which we started this chapter were also used.

They weren't helped by being an "outsider" (from the "wrong" country, the "wrong" university, etc.), but they did also have immense difficulty sharing, be it work, ideas, or praise. They also had immense difficulty delegating and managing their own work, and managing their team of young lawyers. And, finally, they had immense difficulty interacting socially as well as professionally. But they were brilliant. They could dig into a technical issue like no one else, come up with permutations, nuances, answers that no one else could have even conceived might have existed – far less actually been able to produce themselves. So, this colleague was tolerated by others at the firm – if sometimes only barely – for what they added to the bottom line. But they left a trail of wreckage in their wake. Disillusioned and often demotivated subordinates; and deeply irritated colleagues/peers who, burned once too many times, refused to share back with that loner things that they could have clearly added value to (for the simple reason that the experience would have been too painful). And the sad thing was that – to the few who still bothered to look – the loner was quite clearly very unhappy. The whole situation was, in one of the classic business-speak understatements, decidedly suboptimal.

But no one wanted to do anything. It would all be too hard; and anyway, the loner would never change; and, anyway, they really were adding to the bottom line, so why mess with (financial) success? So, the loner got shuffled from one group in the firm to another, until the new set of people got fed up with them, and then they were moved on again. To be very clear, leaving them alone was not "mercy". It was a mixture of laziness and aversion to confrontation on the part of the loner's bosses. So when, eventually, the problem came my way, I decided we really had to try to deal with it (although, at that point, the passing-the-buck approach looked very tempting).

There were three elements to the strategy. First, some open, honest talk; second, a plan to tie what they did much more closely to the overall firm's (team's) goals; and third, over time, an effort to find out a little more what made them a loner. In none of this did I act in an overtly Christian manner (and I wasn't then a priest), but they knew my background, and I think it made them slightly more open to me.

We first had the honest talk, and parts of that weren't fun, but it was clear that the colleague had no idea about the effect they had on those who worked for them, those who worked with them, or, indeed, on some of the firm's clients. It was a true revelation, of an unpleasant variety, but it was a necessary precursor to the second step. We then tried to figure out how, without forcing them to work in a team (square peg; round hole), we could find relatively discrete, separate parts of bigger projects where they could contribute to the larger whole, without having to interact and share in a way that they would have found difficult (or, likely, impossible). We found some enormously technical aspects of certain projects which played directly to their skill-set, and would add greatly to the overall value of the transaction – but which would not hold up the project as a whole while they worked on their particular piece. And we completely took them out of the business of managing the work of more junior lawyers.

The third part involved some personal talks, where I didn't so much ask questions as provide a prompt, followed by some space, to talk about what might be on their mind. So, I would talk about a difficult thing that I had experienced, and see if that found any resonance with them. And slowly, and occasionally, they opened up. A difficulty with a son; worries about other family relationships; a deeply unhappy period in their own adolescence. I won't pretend for a moment that they stopped being a loner, or that they suddenly became happy, but they did begin to trust others a little more to the extent that they would, for example, explain their thinking as they worked on a project. They didn't do this in a way that pulled others into their project, but they did do it in a way that allowed those others to learn from the loner's knowledge and experience and then apply it on their own. And the colleague did also become a little more relaxed, and even, occasionally, smiled...

As a result, that person, our other colleagues, and the workplace as a whole became a slightly more productive, slightly more fulfilled place both for the loner and for others. They didn't become part of the team (and to the best of my knowledge, many years later still have not), but a mixture of honesty, practicality, and a little empathy worked a whole lot better for everyone than either allowing the loner to continue unimpeded, or trying to force them to make themselves into a "team" member. Not a perfect result, but genuine mercy, nevertheless. The loner remained the master of their fate, but, at last, saw a little more clearly that they existed within a larger framework and a larger purpose. To switch metaphors, they ploughed their own furrow, but now understood that they did so within a larger field where others also ploughed, and realized that, together – without any furrows having to overlap – we could all ensure that the whole field would get ploughed.

To return to the passage from Paul, mercy lay in showing the colleague that they didn't have to change from being a foot to being a hand, or try to be the whole body. It's important to note that while Paul was telling the Corinthians that they had come together in the one body of the church through baptism (thus, leaving behind their former separateness), at the same time the body was not a single limb (or member). Paul was actually arguing against conformity inside the church. There was, he said, room for different talents, different characters, different types of people. And it was from diversity inside the one body that real strength, and richness, and fruitful possibility truly lay – so long as everyone understood their common purpose and their common obligation to each other in baptism.

So, to come back to my colleague the loner, they were helped to understand that they could continue to be the distinctive hand they had always been; but they were also helped to understand that while the hand is distinctive, it is also part of a larger body – for the benefit of all – and, therefore, cannot say to the foot or the eye, "I have no need of you."

Being the injured man: accepting mercy

As you'll have gathered, I'm not really much of a loner. I've always worked for large organizations (whether in the public or the private sector), and while teamwork occasionally irritates me – especially if it involves three people working on something where one would be just fine; or involves endless layers of repetitive review – I still know that every single time, the well-run team will produce a better result than will a group of individuals operating independently of each other, however talented they might be.

But there are also downsides to working in such an environment, in that you can become not so much a cog in a machine (although that can happen), as overly reliant on others at the expense of your own initiative. And this, in turn, may mean that however competently you are functioning, you are simply not reaching your full potential. So, let me give you an example of mercy shown to me in this regard. In the law firms in which I'd worked, being given work was generally never a problem (especially late on a Friday afternoon for Monday morning completion); and in the government, within the areas that I covered, there was enough interesting and challenging work for several people. But when I went to GE, my boss made very clear in my job interview that he would not be putting work on my desk. "I'm hiring you to do what needs to be done. You'll figure out what that is. I am not going to tell you what to do. I just hire the right people and then let them get on with it." I found that so odd that I simply didn't believe him. It had to be a recruiting ploy, I decided. An insincere promise, similar to those given at other places where I was interviewing, intended to give me the false illusion of being in charge of my destiny.

But, as it turned out, he wasn't lying. When I went there, the phone didn't ring and nobody walked into my office and put a file on my desk with a string of instructions. It was disconcerting, and for months I wondered why they'd hired me. Eventually, I went back to talk to my boss and said, "You weren't kidding, were you?" "No," came the reply. "So what should I do?" I said. "You'll figure it out," they said. Thanks, boss, I thought. But, eventually, I did. For a year or two it was quite uncomfortable, but slowly I realized that I had, in fact, been given the opportunity and the space to be genuinely creative, to fashion something – in the larger context of the tax team – that was truly my own; to fashion something new through the exercise of whatever gifts I had; to create something that had not been there before. I have, as some of you will recall, always been very rude about the "eat what you kill" mentality of law firms. But there is no doubt that being forced to go out and find your own "food" (with the appropriate support, training, and encouragement) can stretch you, and benefit the workplace, in a way that simply completing other people's projects never can. So, with my boss giving me the financial support, taking a long-term view of the project, and offering enthusiastic encouragement to build a totally new function, I flourished as I hadn't before –

and to the benefit, I hope, of the entire business (the body) and all of my colleagues (its other limbs).

Now, of course, this process could have overshot. The key is to harness and encourage this individuality and creativity within the context of a team and an organization that is all pulling in the same direction and to the same end, and that's not always easy. But I can certainly testify that being forced outside of my comfort zone was – after the initial wobble – an incredibly energizing experience. Initially, it wasn't that easy to go from a place where work was always provided, and the structure of each day, week, month (and perhaps year) was predictable, to somewhere where I really did have to exercise my initiative. But when I began to do it, Henley's words spoke to me. Not because I believed that I'd achieved everything through my own skill and resources; or because I thought I could take everything (or anything) the world threw at me; or because I believed that I could function without the help of others (or of God) at work. I still believed none of those things. *But* being forced to go out on my own gave me, encouraged in me, a creativity that I had begun to doubt was still there. And the more I did, the more I felt I could do. I felt the Holy Spirit at work, that "charism" that Miroslav Volf talks about. I felt, quite simply, a little more alive.

So, I didn't become a loner, but I did become a more creative individual within the team – and in that sense, I did become much more the master of my fate and the captain of my soul. But at the same time, in Paul's terms, while I now saw clearly that I needed to be an authentically individual member of the team – totally identifiably a hand or a foot – I also understood that I was most valuable when I was a fully connected, integrated part of the whole that is the body, the workplace, the community. To be shown that was mercy.

8

THE INSENSITIVE COLLEAGUE

The Pharisees came and began to question Jesus. To test him, they asked him for a sign from heaven. He sighed deeply and said, "Why does this generation ask for a sign? Truly I tell you, no sign will be given to it." Then he left them, got back into the boat and crossed to the other side. The disciples had forgotten to bring bread, except for one loaf they had with them in the boat. "Be careful," Jesus warned them. "Watch out for the yeast of the Pharisees and that of Herod." They discussed this with one another and said, "It is because we have no bread." Aware of their discussion, Jesus asked them: "Why are you talking about having no bread? Do you still not see or understand? Are your hearts hardened? Do you have eyes but fail to see, and ears but fail to hear? And don't you remember? When I broke the five loaves for the five thousand, how many basketfuls of pieces did you pick up?"

"Twelve," they replied. "And when I broke the seven loaves for the four thousand, how many basketfuls of pieces did you pick up?" They answered, "Seven." He said to them, "Do you still not understand?"

Mark 8:11–21 NIV

I have a good friend who was recently told by a guy that she was only 10 pounds (4.5 kg) away from being perfect.

Where on earth do you start with a statement like that? First, it was a comprehensive insult – whatever he thought he might have been saying, what really came out was: "I think you're fat." Second, it was totally sexist. Third, in the age of eating disorders, it was unthinkingly ignorant. Fourth, it trivially equated physical appearance with perfection. And, fifth... well, clearly, I could go on and on, but the bottom line is that it deeply insulted and wounded my friend. And regardless of whether the man was an admirer, a friend, a sibling, or an enemy – and regardless of whether the comment was calculated to hurt, or just plain dumb – that insensitive remark, just as much as the sticks and stones of the childhood rhyme, really, really hurt, deep inside.

Of course, I should admit that my sympathy comes (at least, in part) because I can also be pretty sensitive – not least in an office setting. For example, I find myself wondering for too long whether the (to me) slightly hurtful word that someone else has used is truly a synonym for the gentler, kinder one that I would have used ("unintentional insensitivity", if you will). Or, instead, whether the harshness that I seemed to hear was indeed intended ("intentional insensitivity", perhaps). In work emails, to give another example, my sensitivity to all the possible nuances leads to me spending far too much time pondering the differing implications of various words and phrases that most likely get a five-second glance from their recipient during which they extract the core message, the key fact, or the main "ask". So, perhaps, in fact, I am too sensitive, and far from that sensitivity being a positive in the workplace, or even a neutral, it may actually be a negative – with angst and hand-wringing replacing productive, value-adding work.

Before we go much further, however, we need to ask what "insensitivity" is, and, by extension, who (or what) our insensitive colleague is. It's a term that at its broadest can mean everything and nothing – at its broadest, it can simply be absolutely anything which offends me, or anyone else, regardless of motivation, content, or degree. Yet, at the same time, as we've already seen, insensitivity can be so hurtful and disruptive in the workplace (and elsewhere) that it's worth trying to pin down exactly what it is. So, I want to suggest four types or instances of potential insensitivity in the workplace, and the effects of each of those:

- someone personally insults you intentionally;

- someone blunders carelessly into an issue of great sensitivity to you;

- someone destructively criticizes your work;

- someone criticizes the very nature of the type of work you do.

Obviously, these can be broken down further, and can be delivered with varying degrees of force. But let's stick with the broad outline.

The intentional insult

So, first, the intentional personal insult. To return to the story at the beginning, even in the workplace it can be something as simple as "you're fat", or "you're ugly", or "your breath stinks". These are comments about physical attributes that may be "true" (by the standards of the day), but which are delivered with the intention to hurt. Such comments may be said coldly and with calculation, or angrily in the midst of an argument. I don't intend to spell out the full range of such comments, or all the types of circumstances in which they may be delivered, because, in a way, that's beside the point. The particular comment is less important than the motive and the effect. The motive is to hurt by highlighting a perceived weakness, something about which the other is likely to be sensitive. And the effect is disruption to the balance in the workplace. And, of course, these insults may also relate to work – its quality, or its quantity, or the speed at which it is done – and that may have an even more direct impact on the productivity and atmosphere of the workplace.

Bottom line: one person feels hurt and may either draw back into their shell, or lash out. And fellow workers may also be affected – distressed, angry, themselves left feeling slightly tainted; or, perhaps, encouraged, "liberated" even, to themselves utter such "truths" to others. I'll deal later with what we might do as Christians about this, but this intentional insensitivity can have effects on the speaker, the listener, and on those who hear. It can affect trust between workers in the workplace, their motivation to work, and the whole environment of the workplace. The intentionality of the insult can be like a hammer taken to a piece of china – and, like shattered china, subsequently reconstructing what had previously existed can be very hard.

The unintentional insult

What about unintentional insensitivity? Consider the resident foot-in-mouth expert, or, indeed, the man I described at the beginning of this chapter who managed to offend when delivering what he thought was a compliment. Well, let's expand that a bit. Let's say you're a middle-aged, middle-class, white guy in the office. You may feel you are impeccably fair; indeed you bend over backwards not to offend, and are (secretly) a little put out that you always seem to be the one singled out as being in need of "change". But to someone of a different socio-economic, or racial, or gender background, your "neutral" remarks may feel far from that. Perhaps that's because of the assumptions of privilege – which you think of as normal (normative?) – that are built into your remarks; perhaps that's because of the history (personal or group) that the other person brings to that moment. But without any intention or awareness you have wandered into sensitive territory.

And that's what makes – even with the best will in the world (and sometimes because of it) – unintentional insensitivity, despite much overlapping subject matter (e.g. comments on physical appearance), quite different from intentional insensitivity. That intentional insult has to aim for a known target, because the goal, after all, is to hurt. But unintentional insensitivity can cover a much wider area, precisely because it has no such aim or intentionality. Put differently, how am I to know that bright orange (which I find disgusting) is your favourite colour? Or that you're a lifelong Everton fan when I support the only good team in Liverpool? Or, more seriously, that you are unable to have children, which is, for you, a deep, abiding sorrow that can overwhelm you at even the merest mention? Or that you were abused by a teacher at school, and have memories that are still triggered by the mention of apparently unrelated topics?

And unintentional insensitivity may also take another slightly different form: that of trampling on someone's dreams, perhaps even with the best of intentions. "Be realistic," you say, "don't aim too high." ("Please don't hurt yourself," is what you're thinking.) But maybe that ambition, even if an unrealistic dream, was what got that person through the day; or inspired them to heights they would not have otherwise reached – even if not quite the heights their dreams aspired to.

But we should be aware that unintentional insensitivity, while not intended to wound – not a frontal attack, if you will – is sometimes more devastating than intentional insensitivity because it unwittingly goes into truly secret places, sometimes even places we've tried to hide from ourselves. The unintentional insensitivity finds a chink in our armour and then goes deep inside of us, into the most sensitive, vulnerable places – sometimes into the depths of our soul. We're forced to face, often unexpectedly, our greatest sorrows and greatest fears. And so, in this case, the effect caused by our insensitive colleague is less likely to be anger and tension in the workplace, and more likely to be withdrawal, perhaps deep sadness; a reluctance to engage with our fellow workers, our neighbours, and with the community of the workplace. And that community is diminished, shrunken, by that.

Destructive criticism

The third example of insensitivity is when someone harshly, destructively criticizes your work. You've really put your back into something, you've put in many extra hours, sacrificed the weekend, read and reread it, and you proudly hand it in – only to be summoned back fifteen minutes later and greeted with the words: "This is garbage! Call yourself a lawyer/banker/manager/engineer? You're useless. Get out and do it again. And properly this time." (Seems unlikely? Trust me, it happens...)

Now, there's nothing wrong with robust constructive criticism, and even with your boss expressing frustration. Furthermore, there's a certain management theory that builds this in. A story is told of Henry Kissinger, who was given a paper that a subordinate had slaved over. After an hour, he summoned the subordinate back and told him to rewrite it and bring it back in a week. A week later the scene repeated itself, with Kissinger asking for another rewrite. When the subordinate delivered the third version, Kissinger is reputed to have said: "Now I'll read it." But there is a difference between constructive criticism which aims to build up – or even the Kissinger system, which simply aims for a better-filtered, more considered starting point – and a rant which rocks you back on your heels and makes you feel an inch tall. The effect there is an infusion of fear, arbitrariness, and randomness into the life of the office. It creates doubt that the office is a place where community is being built. And it diminishes the effectiveness of individuals and the team. Fear is a sharp stick, but it does not always drive creativity – sometimes exactly the opposite. And it can make people doubt themselves, become more tentative and less willing to exercise their talents. I can certainly attest that after a few years of that type of environment early in my career, I still doubt my technical competence twenty-five years later...

Criticism of the type of work you do

The final example of insensitivity that I want to look at is when someone questions the very nature of the work you do; your very job itself. Well, fair enough, you might say, immediately thinking of cigarette companies or cluster bomb manufacturers.

But actually, it goes quite a lot wider than that. I can (again) assure you that as a tax guy for a large US multinational I get my share of people asking me how I can do my job (keeping corporate tax low) and still face myself in the mirror in the morning. And, perhaps even more unfortunately, there are plenty of people in the church who take it much broader than that, telling you they cannot imagine why you are working for a profit-making business rather than a charity.

Now, I'm aware that often these people making these comments won't be your colleagues – although plenty of my non-tax colleagues have often looked a little queasy when they hear a media story about tax – but they will often be your peers, and in some cases, those with whom you spend considerable time. Furthermore, this type of criticism impacts the work lives of many people these days across many different types of businesses, from financial services through to pharmaceuticals. And it's important to be aware of it because, in a way, this type of insensitivity can be the worst of the four in its adverse effects on the community of the workplace. It's possible to brush off intentional insensitivity, painful though it may be. Unintentional insensitivity may sometimes go deeper, but at least it doesn't have the wounding intensity of a personal attack. And destructive criticism of our work may be deeply unpleasant and dispiriting, but we can still check it at the door of the office on the way out.

But criticism of the job itself, the totality of what we spend the vast majority of our waking lives doing, is more fundamental. We are, essentially, being told that, at best, we are wasting our lives – and, at worst, that we are actually dedicating our lives and God-given talents to something harmful, something negative, something which may detract from human well-being. "You're wasting your life" is a powerful and wounding message. And it's difficult to hide from. Most of us like to think that we're doing something useful, something meaningful, something beyond simply putting food on the table (not that that is insignificant). So to be told, straight out, that we're wasting our lives diminishes our sense of self-worth and can completely demotivate us, stripping the workplace, the community, the "neighbourhood", of real meaning.

Being the Good Samaritan: showing mercy

In the case of insensitivity of any type, showing "mercy" to those who have been hurt (whether by the "truth" or lies; whether through cruelty or carelessness) is honouring our obligation, our responsibility to offer support, kindness, empathy; to be caring, and build back up what has been broken down. But the purpose of these chapters is to explore how we might show mercy to those who are insensitive (or verbose, or incompetent, etc.) rather than, primarily, to those they affect.

So, how can we show mercy to the insensitive colleague? Here, the too-easy answer is that we need to make them more sensitive. It's the theme of a hundred corporate training courses: demonstrate the fault; show how awful/damaging/ stupid it is; and, once this revelation has been absorbed, people will never be insensitive again. (Except, of course, they will.) It's a variation on the Golden Rule – if only you can show people what they are actually doing unto others, and how little they would like it done unto themselves, then surely they'll stop. The trouble is, there's something a little preachy about the Golden Rule, which distances it from real life. Yes, yes, everyone agrees, of course we'd never do that – but it has that bifurcated church-on-Sunday-work-on-Monday feel to it, which means that it doesn't seem to apply at work during the week.

Showing mercy: using "confrontation"

So, I want to suggest instead that this mercy may sometimes come through confrontation (although I need to explain that word) – something that gets below the surface, rather than papers over the cracks. What I mean by "confrontation" is both sides meeting together and being honest with each other. It's the essence of mediation – from marriage guidance counselling for couples, to large-scale truth and reconciliation commissions for nations. It's the idea that by very carefully, and in a controlled way, letting the other side know the hurt that you are feeling, you can bring that hurt to an end (or at least to a place where you can deal with it, without it poisoning relationships).

Let me try to illustrate with an example that relates to the fourth type of insensitivity. In that case, the effect on work and a workplace of being told that you're engaged in negative rather than positive activity can be deeply dispiriting and needs addressing. So, how could we show mercy through "confrontation" to the person delivering the criticism? Well, occasionally I get a group of business and NGO tax people together to talk about tax and development. Such meetings can be dialogues of the deaf, with the business folks dismissing the NGOs as lacking sufficient tax expertise to hold a sensible conversation, and the NGOs dismissing the business folks as wilfully concentrating on the details in order to avoid facing up to the bigger picture (and the threat to their jobs and livelihoods). But, as emerged in a few of these meetings, expressing these views caused considerable hurt on both sides that damaged trust and the possibility of fruitful dialogue.

Why all that hurt? Well, think about how each side viewed itself. On the one hand, when, as a business tax person, you sit in an office staring at the tax code all day, thinking you are just helping your business carry on as efficiently as possible, it's really quite hurtful to be accused of harming starving babies in Africa. And that is often made worse when there is a story in the *Guardian* or *New York Times*, and a friend, or a member of your church, asks you how you as a Christian (or a human being) can live with your conscience. On the other hand, the NGOs have been, in turn, accused of finding a subject with resonance ("tax kills babies"), and milking it cynically as a fundraising tool. That is very hurtful, too. So, I suggested to the group that we spend the evening talking not about facts and figures, or theories and policies, but about how it felt to be insensitively (and unfairly) attacked for the thing, the job, to which we devoted so much time, so much of our life. How it felt to be told as a business person that you were harming starving babies in order to lead a comfortable, first-world life in London. How it felt to be told as an NGO that you didn't really care about any specific topic independent of its ability to raise funds to keep you and your friends feeling good about yourselves while you zipped around the global south in white Toyota Land Cruisers.

Don't tell me what you think, I asked, tell me what you *feel*. And in that neutral space of St Martin's, a lot of hurt flowed out on both sides. From tax professionals: decent people who had been trained as experts, trying to ensure their businesses didn't walk into tax bear traps, while – yes – taking advantage of breaks that the law offered, and in doing both, helping their businesses be more effective in fulfilling a mission which they believed benefited society. And from NGO/aid workers: decent people who had forgone private sector salaries, and had endured being told that they never knew what they were talking about, in order to raise the profile of a subject (tax) that they thought central to development issues. It wasn't a big thing, but by confronting one side with evidence of the emotional impact of their insensitivity on the other, it was possible to build up a level of trust and appreciation for the other. And it has allowed since then for a creativity in trying to craft solutions that insensitivity and hurt would otherwise have prevented.

So, while sensitivity training (on race, gender, sexual harassment, treating your employees properly, and so many other topics) will always be important in helping to prevent intentional and unintentional insensitivity, true mercy may need something different. Whether you call it mediation, or conciliation, or neutral space, it's about providing a place where both sides can, first, pull back without "losing", and then move forward without "giving in". A place where heart is as important as head, because the insensitive person needs not only to logically understand the insensitivity with their head, but also feel the power of that insensitivity with their heart. To understand what their insensitivity has done to another person; how it has hurt; how it may have shaken something that is at the very core of the other person.

Now, perhaps what I tried with that NGO/business group can't be directly replicated in every office setting, but other types of mediated forums in the workplace – run by HR or outsiders – may bring that change of heart (rather than simply of head; and achieve that through understanding rather than fear of disciplinary action) that can transform the insensitive colleague's life, and the life of the office. It can be equally applied in one-on-one or in group settings. And it can be applied to intentional and unintentional insensitivity, and to destructive criticism, as well as to criticism of the job itself.

One of my favourite quotations is from the American poet Henry Wadsworth Longfellow, who said: "My enemy is the man [person] whose story I do not know." In a situation of controlled "confrontation" that story can emerge, those enmities can be defused, and new creativity and community can develop.

Being the injured man: accepting mercy

Earlier, I said that as a privileged, white, middle-class male, I could be blind to all sorts of insensitivities because of my status-quo view of what was normative. But even before that, I said that I could be sensitive, perhaps overly sensitive, worrying about the shades of meanings of a word – whether used by me, or applied to me – to a level that struck some as going beyond sensitivity, and on into neuralgia. To be sure, at one level this can be easily explained because as humans what we do to others often begins to feel very different when others do it to us. But I think there's a bit more going on. There is a real danger that our own sensitivity may become insensitivity towards other people. That might be a lack of openness to their needs because we spend so much time worrying about our own sensitivities. Or it might be a feeling, belief almost, that because we are so careful, so sensitive in one area, it's quite impossible that we could be insensitive in others.

I'm aware that all sounds paradoxical (or, perhaps, plain incomprehensible) so let me have another go. Part of our insensitivity is caused by our sensitivity – that is, we become so wrapped up in ourselves that we fail to notice what others need. And this can play out in several ways. In the most benign case, we end up simply assuming that everyone shares our sensitivities and we, therefore, minister to other people assuming they have our needs, rather than trying to discover what theirs might be. Second, we may become so wrapped up in ourselves that we simply don't have/make/find the time to look after others. Or, third, and definitely worst, we may try to make ourselves feel better by sharing, and thereby, transferring, our sensitivities (and, often, insecurities) with/to others.

In the opening passage from Mark, Jesus treats the disciples harshly, perhaps even insensitively. They are having trouble being anything other than literal – but, you might think, He's the Son of God and they are humble artisans. They can't be expected to understand everything. However, the point Jesus is making here is that it is the disciples themselves who are being insensitive. Despite all of the new evidence in front of their eyes, of the miraculous things done in their sight, they cannot break out of their old way of thinking. Their hearts are hardened. They are being literal when He is being metaphorical. And despite having seen His glory in the miracles of feeding the 5,000 and 4,000, as well as the truculence of the scribes and Pharisees, they remain insensitive to both experiences. So, to make them more sensitive to the new reality that is before them, Jesus must Himself be less sensitive. The Jesus who saves sinners, who will not condemn adulterers, who dines with tax collectors and prostitutes, and who is all love and little judgment, will, nevertheless, use insensitivity to those closest to Him when necessary. "Do you have eyes but fail to see, and ears but fail to hear?"

So, following on from this, mercy to me, as the injured man, may sometimes be someone saying: "Snap out of it. Stop overthinking this. Stop examining every tiny nuance. Stop looking inwards. Don't be self-indulgent. Concentrate on what's really important." And that has two related but connected benefits. First, I will focus again on what others really need, and what the bigger picture is. And, second, I will stop focusing on myself so much; will stop focusing exclusively on my own needs, concerns, and neuroses. Of course, this "mercy" must be given carefully, and with love – not out of a desire to wound, or to inflict pain, or to deliver judgment.

Let me give a couple of examples. I go for spiritual direction every couple of months, and my spiritual director almost always asks tough, difficult – some might call them insensitive – questions to shake me out of a certain comfortable way of thinking. The questions are intended – out of love – to cut fairly close to the bone, in order to shake my thinking out of the safe, conventional ruts into which my sensitivities have deposited it. Theology, ethics, work, family: nothing is off limits. And all benefit me through an increased sensitivity to others produced by a dose of calculated, loving insensitivity from him. "Are your hearts hardened?"

And another example. Fairly recently my (secular) boss asked me to do something and not be afraid to tread on people's toes in doing so. I must have looked somewhat dubious, so my boss explained: "You worry too much sometimes about what other people think, and what their turf is. What's important here is what's best for the team and the company as a whole. That may require you to tread on other people's toes. So that's exactly what I'm asking you to do." I was a little taken aback, but when I had thought it through, I realized that my sensitivity had become insensitivity – my fear of offending others; and indeed, of being offended myself – and it required a little insensitivity to pull me back. I needed to be told, I needed to be shaken into realizing that the good of the business, the joint endeavour in which we were all engaged, required me to put aside the numerous and minute gradations of nuance that comforted my conscience, and be sensitive to a (larger) need that was not my own.

And, finally, I had another colleague who used to give a talk on "succeeding at work". All of his points were good, some straightforward, some surprising. But the one that struck me came towards the end of his talk and (slightly cleaned up for this book) it was: "Never be a bigger pain in the rear than you have to be." The advice is useful because, first, it acts as a limit on what you do in the workplace, including those times when you need to be (lovingly, but intentionally) insensitive. It also says, however, that there can be a place for being a pain, for being insensitive. For the good of the individual, for the good of the group, for the good of the workplace, sometimes you may need to be a pain, in order to right the balance again. For someone like me, that is mercy. Not because it tells me that I have permission to be insensitive anytime I want to be; but rather because it tells me that sometimes I must be insensitive even when I really don't want to be.

9

THE OPTIMISTIC COLLEAGUE

But Jehoshaphat also said to the king of Israel, "Inquire first for the word of the Lord." Then the king of Israel gathered the prophets together, about four hundred of them, and said to them, "Shall I go to battle against Ramoth-gilead, or shall I refrain?" They said, "Go up; for the Lord will give it into the hand of the king." But Jehoshaphat said, "Is there no other prophet of the Lord here of whom we may inquire?" The king of Israel said to Jehoshaphat, "There is still one other by whom we may inquire of the Lord, Micaiah son of Imlah; but I hate him, for he never prophesies anything favourable about me, but only disaster."… The messenger who had gone to summon Micaiah said to him, "Look, the words of the prophets with one accord are favourable to the king; let your word be like the word of one of them, and speak favourably." But Micaiah said, "As the Lord lives, whatever the Lord says to me, that I will speak."

When he had come to the king, the king said to him, "Micaiah, shall we go to Ramoth-gilead to battle, or shall we refrain?" He answered him, "Go up and triumph; the Lord will give it into the hand of the king." But the king said to him, "How many times must I make you swear to tell me nothing but the truth in the name of the Lord?" Then Micaiah said, "I saw all Israel scattered on the mountains, like sheep that have no shepherd; and the Lord said, 'These have no master; let each one go home in peace.'" The king of Israel said to Jehoshaphat, "Did I not tell you that he would not prophesy anything favourable about me, but only disaster?"... The king of Israel then ordered, "Take Micaiah, and return him to Amon the governor of the city and to Joash the king's son, and say, 'Thus says the king: Put this fellow in prison, and feed him on reduced rations of bread and water until I come in peace.'"

1 Kings 22:5–8, 13–18, 26–27 NRSV

Pollyanna Whittier was a young girl with golden curls and a winning smile in the 1913 book by the American author Eleanor Porter. Incurably optimistic, despite being an orphan, Pollyanna played something she called the "glad game" where she would first find, and then celebrate, the silver lining of every dark cloud that came her way. Slowly she turned around not just her slightly dour spinster aunt, but also the entire disheartened New England town in which she lived. And over the intervening hundred years her name has given rise to adjectival and adverbial forms – such as "Pollyannaish" – which, it has to be said, are not always used with total approbation.

I have neither golden curls, nor a particularly winning smile, and yet I do like to think Pollyanna and I have something in common. Let me explain. With one of the tax groups that I chair, I know that the subjects up for discussion – governments cracking down on tax avoidance in international transactions with a myriad of new rules – will often provoke strong feelings. So, before we start, I try to break the ice and defuse some of that tension that I know is swirling around by saying something along the lines of: "As I was coming here this morning, I was trying to figure out whether to be Pollyanna, or Oscar the Grouch."[18] It usually provokes a few smiles, and elicits a few groans (so at least the ice is broken, if not the tension defused) and I then go on to say, "and I decided that today, I am going to be Pollyanna." I then give as upbeat an assessment as I feel I can – without getting lynched by my peers – of where the business community stands on the particular issue we are discussing. And as I go through this routine, one of my favourite, much-repeated (and Pollyannaish) phrases, after I've explained the potentially negative implications of any measure, is to say "but the good news is..." It's a habit that I know drives some people mad. And I will also grant that I do tend to deal with some problems by simply ignoring them and their implications. But my experience is that it's generally not too difficult to identify and then dwell (wallow, perhaps) in the negatives. However, that's rarely the way forward. At least, to my way of thinking, a little bit of sunniness can go a long way in helping people to reach productive solutions.

And, anyway, what's wrong with a little bit of optimism, you might ask? Given the ability of most people to spend much of their time grumbling about much of what goes on

---

18 For those of you who aren't Muppets fans, Oscar the Grouch is a puppet (Muppet) from the children's TV show, *Sesame Street*, who lives in a dustbin/garbage can, and is remarkably grumpy and most decidedly not optimistic.

in the workplace, what's wrong with a little bit of sunniness? Doesn't that help the cohesion in the workplace that we say we're looking for – and which is part of God's purpose, no less, in creating a community? Doesn't it help people realize more of their potential, find their charism, and work in the Spirit towards the healing of creation? Yes, you might say, you can see how the lazy or incompetent or insensitive colleague might have an impact, and might benefit from "mercy". But the optimist – really?

Well, let's look a little more closely at what optimism is, and what the problems might be. The dictionary definitions are actually quite illuminating – although not for entirely straightforward reasons. They seem to coalesce around two or three meanings:

- a disposition to hope for the best, or to look on the bright side of things under all circumstances;

- the doctrine that this world is the best of all possible worlds;

- the belief that good must ultimately prevail over evil.

The first is Pollyanna's sunniness that I referred to earlier, but the other two have some interesting implications that we'll look at in a little more detail when we come to "mercy". The premise of this chapter, however, is that our optimistic colleague can be a problem. So, I want to start in a slightly different place to the dictionary, by assuming that the optimism has already led to disaster – or, at least, a less than desirable outcome – and examine instead the roots of the (over) optimism that led to the result. And to do that I think we need to look at three possible roots of that optimism: arrogance, laziness, and blindness.

Arrogant optimism

The CEO

First, "arrogant optimism". There's the obvious – but nevertheless not wholly inaccurate – stereotype of the cigar-chewing megalomaniac business tycoon, usually a man, who (over) confidently assumes that all problems will disappear before his genius/experience/forceful personality. This boss may think that he (and, probably, he alone) can weld together two completely different corporate cultures in a megadeal that the world (or, at least, the City/Wall Street) will swoon over. No matter that one organization is essentially bureaucratic and the other entrepreneurial; or that one is hierarchical and the other flat; or that different languages and national cultures are involved; or that the IT and ERP systems are totally incompatible. The boss is supremely confident he can sweep those issues aside. Or a variant on this: the boss keeps acquiring disparate business lines confident that he alone can weld them into a single unit, defying the almost universal rule that conglomerates fail.[19]

Because the boss is who he is, he, arrogantly and optimistically, believes and asserts he can bulldoze through these problems through sheer force of personality – preferably with some Churchillian quote on his lips: "Difficulties mastered are opportunities won"; or, perhaps, "Never, never, never give in"; or, most appositely for this subject: "A pessimist sees the difficulty in every opportunity; an optimist sees the opportunity in every difficulty." Stirring stuff, to be sure, but, as a friendly critic once noted, Churchill's language tended to: "soar above the sober and often intransigent facts of reality".[20]

19 I realize as a (soon-to-be former) employee of General Electric I am treading on dangerous ground. But most groups with multiple business lines struggle to find the economic coherence and synergies that are advertised/assumed at the time of the acquisition of those disparate businesses.

20 Jan Smuts, the South African general and political ally of Churchill.

That reality is that some things won't work; and other things can't work. Sometimes hard toil, strenuous exertion, and sheer grind can pull off an unlikely success. But sunny (arrogant) optimism alone won't. Indeed, one of the major problems of this type of I-can-do-anything optimism is that it often precludes the detailed planning and the deep realism necessary to weather setbacks. And this lack of planning thereby dooms what would always, at the best of times, have been a difficult project, before it has even begun.

The middle manager

While we may all end up bearing the burden of the CEO's arrogance, most of us aren't CEOs, or even in regular contact with them. Nevertheless, this type of arrogant optimism equally exists in slightly different forms lower down in the workplace hierarchy. Think, for example, of the mid-level manager who assumes that they can train any person to fill a certain role, thus leading them to hire someone otherwise unsuited to the job who has impressed them for some tangential reason. As, when getting married, you should never assume that you can change someone's fundamental characteristics because they love you; nor, when hiring someone for a job, should you assume you can change those characteristics simply because you pay them. The effect may be on a smaller scale than with the CEO, but the result is similar. Someone inappropriate is hired, much effort and angst are then put into trying to change them (in itself creating tension), the work doesn't get done properly, other people have to carry the load – and all because the manager assumed that they could do what no one else could do.

Or consider a departmental restructuring (upsizing or downsizing) based on a management theory designed for a different type of business which the manager is nevertheless convinced that they (and they alone) can make work. The result? Again, much effort may be put into forcing square pegs into round holes. If upsizing, people are hired only to become quickly dissatisfied. If downsizing, people are let go, creating gigantic holes in the fabric of the department. And, eventually, when the extent of the over-optimism becomes clear, a lot of effort then has to be devoted to putting Humpty-Dumpty back together again.

Me

This arrogant optimism may not just be the failing of our boss. It may also be our own failing, and can take several different forms. I know from my own experience that if someone offers me an interesting work assignment, or an interesting project at church, or an outside role in an interesting organization, then I'll say yes on the basis that, while I know I already have too much on my plate, "somehow I'll make it work". Now, this may sound admirable, almost worthy, and, perhaps, even endearing – but, at a certain point, it really isn't. Because the reality is that once my time is full up, it's full up. So, despite my assumption (honestly and sincerely held though it may be) that I can do it all, even if others couldn't, in reality at least some of it won't get done well. This may not have the catastrophic consequences of the boss who runs a business employing tens of thousands, or even the mid-level manager who makes a misery of the lives of the fifteen people who work for them. But it will still harm the work I have taken on (and, thus, God's creation). And it will also put strains on me that may affect every aspect of my life – creativity, time with my family, time with God.

Arrogant optimism in all its forms is one of the dark sides of Pollyanna – and that's a problem.

Lazy optimism

Next there's lazy optimism. Now, clearly, there's some overlap between arrogant optimism and lazy optimism (and blind optimism). But there are also differences, depending on whether arrogance, laziness, or blindness is the predominant characteristic. If lazy does predominate, then there may still be several subcategories, but what links them all is a lack of attention to, a lack of interest in, a lack of belief in the importance of detail. Let me tell a few stories.

"Good enough"

When I worked for the US Treasury we had a saying that when we got something (a regulation, a legislative proposal, a budget estimate) to a certain point of development, then it was "good enough for government work", and we could stop working on that and move on to the next project. Now at one level that was simply a variant on a more acceptable maxim: "don't let the perfect be the enemy of the good". (In other words, to get through the never-ending workload you can't carry on polishing everything to the Nth degree – you get it to "good enough" and move on.) But while this could well have been "lazy" in its lack of attention to detail, was it also "optimistic"? I think so, because what really underlay our assumption that what we had done was "good enough" was a belief that nothing could (or would) go wrong as a result – because it hadn't before. So instead of doing everything we could, we did just about "enough" on the basis that nothing could really go wrong. And, of course, usually it didn't. But I do remember one set of tax regulations rushed through because they were high profile (that should have sent up a warning flag right there...) despite it being obvious that not everything completely joined up, that not every possible set of circumstances had been covered, that not every possible

146

problem had been anticipated. It quickly became clear that far from being "good enough" the regulations were actually severely deficient – and not just the draftsperson, but several of my colleagues had to spend months cleaning up and "retrofitting" the regs. There was, to be sure, an element of arrogant optimism in that – but there was also quite a lot of lazy optimism.

Everything worked out in the past

To give another example, I've already mentioned how I and my fellow students at university were, by some standards, rather lazy. There were various reasons for this: some people saw this as their last (three-year) opportunity to do the bare minimum; for others, it was what I have called the myth of "effortless ease"; and still others were not so much lazy, as incapable of dealing with the total lack of structure after years of intensively structured secondary education, and so, effectively, gave up. But what underlay all of these – and what prevented widespread panic – was also an optimism that, because we were where we were, because we'd worked hard to get there (we liked to tell ourselves), and because our predecessors seemed to have done all right, then, well, we'd probably do all right, too. As it turned out some did (although often they worked harder than they would ever admit to), but some didn't. And that was a waste – of talent, of opportunity, and of the "future". Of course, some might call this a "sense of entitlement" rather than optimism, and, in some cases, that was undoubtedly true. But this attitude spread far beyond those born with silver spoons in their mouths. And the attitude was, in the end, more facile than entitled. A sense that things had gone well in the past, and so they also would in the future. A sense that the past had been golden, so that the future also had to be. It is a mistake that we keep making, because often it is easier, and more pleasant, than facing reality.

It's never gone wrong before

To give a final example of lazy optimism, back in the workplace, assume that regulation in your industry is becoming tighter and tighter, the relevant government authorities more rigorous in their examinations, and public and media attention much more focused on your line of business. And yet your boss, or your compliance colleague, on the basis that the business has never been caught/audited/featured in the press before, takes the view that you'll all be able to muddle through because you never do anything wrong. It may well be true that you never do anything wrong, but in the new environment that may not be enough. You may have to prove that you had control procedures in place to make sure nothing went wrong; you may need documentary evidence that you did things right. But, instead, you lazily extrapolate out from the past, and then when lightning strikes, you are totally unprepared and the business is seriously damaged.

Blind optimism

The third type of optimism that I identified, blind optimism, shares some features with the lazy variety. But it also differs in that there is more of a wilfulness to it. There is an active element that differentiates it from the passivity of lazy optimism. There is still something mildly endearing about a *Brideshead Revisited* type of lazy optimism – that ethereal, dreamlike place where a languid, golden summer sun forever shines. Blind optimism, by contrast, is the refusal to acknowledge that the brick wall you are heading towards at 70 mph is a brick wall; or even, while you admit it is a brick wall, you still refuse to acknowledge that you'll actually hit it; or even, while you admit you will hit it, you still refuse to acknowledge that hitting it could ever do you and your vehicle any damage. It is, in short, the ignoring of inconvenient facts that contradict the story you have decided you want to tell.

This time it's (not) different

At the macro level the financial crisis of 2007/08 gives us numerous examples of blind optimism. And again, here there is an overlap with the arrogant and lazy optimisms, but the blindness is to the fore. It's less about super-boss defying the odds, or someone lazily assuming that nothing can go wrong because nothing has before. It's more the idea that despite the clear risks, and despite the lessons of the past, this time the obvious, the inevitable, simply won't happen. To use the phrase spoken confidently in the years leading up to the financial crisis (and used more ironically since): "This time it's different." This time (they said) the laws of gravity, the laws of probability have been suspended, and what goes up need not come down. Furthermore, and unlike arrogant optimism, which is often about the individual ego, this type of blind optimism often springs from "groupthink" and conventional wisdom (where it can, obviously, overlap again with laziness).

To illustrate: the original inventors of the financial instruments that precipitated the crash, such as Collateralized Debt Obligations and Credit Default Swaps, may have been arrogantly optimistic "Masters of the Universe" who thought they could change the world. But most of those who were involved as sellers and purchasers (as detailed by Michael Lewis in *The Big Short*) were those who simply closed their eyes to logic, to past experience, and to the proven adage that "if it's too good to be true, then it probably is..." The laws of finance may not be quite as rigid as the iron laws of physics, but they do still hold. Thus, for example, too much money chasing too few assets will lead to inflated asset prices and to a bubble that will eventually deflate. And another: junk assets rated AAA are still junk assets. As the financial crisis showed, we had not "eliminated the cycle of boom and bust". And as the financial crisis also showed in relation to far too much corporate borrowing, in relation to far too much lending to risky borrowers, and in relation to far too little due diligence on the CDOs by bankers, blindness simply doesn't work because it was not – and never is – completely "different this time". It was a brick wall up ahead; we were going to hit it; and when we hit it, we were going to do ourselves and our vehicle a lot of damage. It was never going to be "different this time".

I'm not going to let the facts cloud my judgment

And to take this down to more micro examples in the office, we've already talked about the bad hire. That may be arrogant optimism – "I (and only I) can change this person." But, just as likely, it's blindness: that character trait doesn't really matter; or we can work around that potential flaw; or that person will fit in eventually. We see what we want to see, and hear what we want to hear, filtering out those things that don't match the mental template we've constructed. I'm as guilty (or capable) of this as everyone else, but I once learned a valuable lesson being on the other end. In additional to the physical, business-wrecking results of optimism visited on others, there is often also a personal detriment to the optimist. And that's because all types of optimism, but perhaps, particularly, blind optimism, can (to adapt Oscar Wilde's aphorism) curdle and sour into cynicism.

I was once interviewed for a job where the law firm was looking for somebody with a sub-specialism in a certain type of financial instrument. I had had some (minimal) exposure to this type of instrument at a previous firm, so, when asked if I had such experience, I said "yes". I interview well, and have a good CV/resume, so that was that, and I got the job.

Within six months, when it had become clear that I didn't have that specialized experience, things had started to go rapidly downhill. I was accused of lying in my interview; my referees were accused of inaccuracies or exaggerations in their references. Perhaps I should have been clearer about the minimal nature of my experience (and, believe me, in every interview since then I have been *crystal* clear about what I don't know, as well as about what I do). But the real culprit was blind optimism. I was coming from a firm that had no reputation for that type of work, and my CV/resume did not list it among the things I had worked on. Harder questions should have been asked – to which I would have given truthful answers. But they weren't asked. The interviewers saw what they wanted to see, and heard what they wanted to hear – against the evidence, or, at the very least, without probing it too hard. And the inevitable result was at least two sets of unhappy people: me and the people who had interviewed and hired me – with the disruptive results rippling out across (and indeed beyond) the workplace. The grain fields of the Lord were heavy with the harvest; God's fractured creation was yearning to be healed. But, instead, both were damaged by the carelessness that is optimism.

The problem with not listening to Micaiah…

There are many stories in the Bible about optimism, but few which combine arrogant, lazy, and blind optimism in the way that the story of the battle between Ahab, King of Israel, his ally, Jehoshaphat, King of Judah, and the Arameans does. There is the groupthink in the lazy optimism of the 400 prophets: "Of course, you'll win, great king. The Lord will give them into your hands!" There is the arrogant optimism of Ahab who tells Jehoshaphat how he hates Micaiah for always giving bad (i.e. realistic) news. So, Ahab ignores Micaiah, tossing him into jail for his unwelcome prophecy, thus simply and arrogantly assuming that he knows better than God's prophet. And then there is Ahab's blind optimism (shared, one presumes, by his commanders) that his ruse of dressing as an ordinary soldier will keep him safe in the heat of battle. It's worked before, perhaps, so why not this time? But an arrow finds Ahab anyway, and that's that. Optimism in all its forms, all totally unjustified, lays Israel and its people low. The message is pretty clear.

Of course, there are similar stories, if not on such a scale, in the New Testament. The arrogant optimism of the Pharisees that they had been blessed with wisdom and goodness. The blind optimism of the high priests that they could satisfy both the Romans and God. The lazy optimism of so many in Israel that God would rescue them from the bind they were in by sending a Messiah who would lead an improbable revolt, and wave a magic wand to make all their physical trouble and spiritual emptiness go away. Facile optimism in each case was substituted for deep hope.

The Bible is pretty clear: optimism can be a problem.

Being the Good Samaritan: showing mercy

There is an obvious, but unfortunately also very smug, way to show "mercy" to our optimistic colleague of whatever variety (although if the colleague is the arrogantly optimistic CEO, discretion may still be the better part of valour). All involve the delivery of sensible home truths on the dangers of optimism, all of them underpinned by the fact that we are a more realistic, more responsible, more far-sighted, more balanced, basically better human being than our colleague. But, of course, that's not really mercy – either to the person lying in the road, or to ourselves. It's just another variation on the Luke 18 Pharisee praying next to the tax collector: "God, I thank you that I am not like other people..." (verse 11 NRSV). No, as ever, mercy will have to lie somewhere other than demonstrating that we are the role model bountifully dispensing the truth. Mercy involves binding up the wounds of the injured, not rubbing salt into them while feeling good about ourselves.

Mercy: arrogance

So, what might mercy to the arrogant optimist look like? Well, given certain aspects of their personality, as I've just said, simply suggesting they are speeding down the road towards inevitable disaster may not work. It is, of course, gently worth probing the arrogance to find its root. Is it deep-seated, or is it a reaction, or a front, to cover up insecurity in their work life, or their personal life? If it is these latter, then there is the possibility of helping, gently, to sort out some of the underlying issues and thereby also solving the arrogant optimism. But if the arrogance is more deep-seated, something at the heart of that person, then something else is needed. I have mentioned before (in Chapter 7) the possibility of deflecting or subverting a problem (or a temptation) by working with its grain, rather than openly opposing it,[21] so let's consider that here.

How might that work? Well, you might tell the CEO that you think he's brilliant, his plan is beyond superlatives, and you just want to be there at his right hand to observe its glorious conclusion. Once you've flattered your way into a position of influence, you can then seek to gently subvert or deflect the worst aspects of the plans, perhaps by gently pointing out flaws and suggesting potential solutions (which, laying aside your own ego, become, of course, the boss's own bright and original idea...). Or perhaps you do the number crunching

---

21 This is derived from Sam Wells' idea of "over-accepting" in *Improvisation: The Drama of Christian Ethics* (Brazos Press, 2004).

and scenario planning that the egotistical boss fails to do, so that you increase the project's chance of success. Or perhaps you can even suggest something even more ambitious (and totally ludicrous) so that the boss revisits his own original idea. ("Boss, your idea to increase our borrowings by £100 million is brilliant but would be even more brilliant at £200 million. Putting aside the slightly greater than 50% risk of total wipeout, here's how much we could make if all the stars line up in a once-in-a-millennium alignment…") You may not be able to change course completely, but even a 5-degree change in direction over a long distance can make a big difference.

And likewise, at the micro level. Get yourself involved in the hiring process; get yourself involved in the departmental reorganization process so that you can subvert it slightly, deflect it to a better place. In every case, however, mercy to the arrogant will not be telling them they are arrogant and pointing out the disadvantages of that; but, rather, it will be helping them realize that themselves, or, by gentle deflection, helping them to a position where they can do less damage to themselves and others.

Mercy: laziness

What about lazy optimists? Mercy here will be slightly different, but, equally, will not come from telling them they are lazy. Again, we should seek to gently subvert, rather than openly confront. In the government example that I gave, you could turn that into a story against yourself, by recounting how your own "good enough for government work" attitude had once, and spectacularly, backfired. By making the story about yourself and your failings, you allow others to feel good (and maybe even slightly superior) about leaving their own problems behind. And if this sounds (as it may also have done in relation to arrogant optimism) ever-so-slightly deceitful, then remember what Jesus said about being both as wise/cunning as serpents, in addition to being innocent as doves. Flattery, and telling a parable, can be both innocent and cunning.

But there's also another way of showing mercy to the lazy optimist. Lazy optimism is, perhaps, at its root, a lack of attention. Arrogant and blind optimism may wilfully ignore, or arrogantly dismiss inconvenient details; but lazy optimism can't even be bothered to find them out in the first place. There's an interesting question as to whether the laziness is born of optimism ("Things will always work out, so why sweat the details?"), or if the optimism is born of laziness ("I can't be bothered to look at this too hard, so I'll assume everything will be fine"). In either case, there is a lazy lack of attention. So, mercy to the lazy optimist may be to work with them, and pay great attention both to the work you are doing together and also to them. You do the former to show them how very close attention removes the need to rely on shallow optimism. And you do the latter because if you pay attention to them, they may begin to pay attention to you, and to others, and the laziness (which can also rest on the lazy optimist hoping/ knowing others will clean up after them) may lessen.

Mercy: blindness

Finally, blind optimism: what would be mercy there? As with arrogant optimism, it may be placing yourself in a position where you can gently divert the situation away from the looming disaster by planning meticulously for its aftermath, or by trying to avert it. And with blind optimism, which often comes from groupthink and conventional wisdom, it may be possible to more directly criticize that groupthink without directly attacking your colleague. For example, you can do that by simply arguing that it isn't "different this time", because it never is. But I also need to acknowledge here that sometimes it may not be that easy. Sometimes you may need to tell people that they are making a massive mistake – that's what Micaiah did, and, as with him, you needn't expect short-term thanks from your optimistic colleague. But it may still be the right thing to do.

And, another thing which could be mercy, although also bringing you some short-term pain, is when you, as the object of the story, close that story down. For example, I would have saved everyone a lot of trouble in that job interview I mentioned earlier if I'd made clear to my (blindly optimistic) interviewers my minimal experience in the area they were interested in. I could have hammered it home by saying, "Look, I know you really want to hear that I can do XYZ, but you need to realize that's NOT what I'm saying." You/I might not get the job, but the interviewers, the business, and you/I would all be better off as a result of honesty and realism over blind optimism. (And I really have been much more prepared to challenge blind optimism ever since – as those who know me well can testify, I really *can* be Oscar the Grouch as well as Pollyanna!)

Being the injured man: accepting mercy

After spending some time talking about showing mercy to our optimistic colleague, the obvious reversal in this section would be to talk about how a little optimism makes the world go around – essentially the story I told at the beginning. About gaining the right perspective on whether the glass is half full, or half empty; about holding an appropriate balance between realism and optimism. But I'm not going to go down that route, because I think it misses a crucial point. In our lives, the question is not whether the glass is half-full or half-empty, but, rather, who fills the glass. Is it us or God? Because it's that that makes the real difference.

My spiritual director spends quite a lot of his time with me getting slightly annoyed at stories like the one I opened with, and for two reasons. First, it does show a certain cast of mind towards a sunny optimism which belies the facts. But, second, and just as importantly, because it shows me in charge of events. Yes, things are a bit sticky; yes, people are being a bit difficult; yes, there are storm clouds on the horizon (or even overhead). But, nevertheless, in the midst of all this – in my version of the narrative of my life – I'm in control of myself and, to some extent, events. Everything (sort of) hangs together, and everything can be sorted out in the end. And he pins this fault – or, rather, both of them – at their root, on an ancient heresy known as Pelagianism.

In very rough terms, Pelagius (a contemporary of, and deeply disliked by, St Augustine of Hippo) did not believe that the world is inherently bad and that humans are inevitably doomed to be sinful. Rather, he argued, while it may be difficult, we have the capacity inside ourselves to be good, and through our own effort, and with encouragement from others, that good can win out. Well, you might say, that's a little Pollyannaish, perhaps, but not a bad approach to take. In fact, however, and as I have come to realize, it is actually a really bad approach – because it means we think we really can do it all alone, without God's help. And that is optimism, pure and simple: lazy, blind, and arrogant. It may work when the sun shines – as optimism does – but not when the storm comes, and the waters rise. Then (to use a different parable-based metaphor) we need firmer foundations than optimism and belief in ourselves can ever provide. We need a rock on which to build. A rock that can withstand the shattering of illusions about our own ability to control the situation; can withstand the shattering of illusions about the general "goodness" of our fellow humans; and, most importantly, can withstand the shattering of illusions about our own inherent goodness. Mercy to us, as we lie in the gutter with that glass lying next to us – no longer half-full or half-empty, because it is broken in a thousand pieces – comes in understanding that although we seem to have been abandoned by Lady Luck, although the world appears to have rejected us, and although we loathe ourselves, all of those are matters of little or no consequence. Because God still loves us. Because God will pick us up if we let Him. And because God will give us another glass, which He will fill (again and again). Augustine often appears as Oscar the Grouch to Pelagius's Pollyanna. But Augustine's insistence that it is by God's grace alone, rather than our own human endeavour, that good things will (sometimes only eventually, but, nevertheless, always) come, gives us the strength and hope that the future will be better in the way that optimism, tempered or otherwise, never can.

So, mercy for me, lying in the road, is being weaned away from an idea that I'm in control, and an idea that goodness will prevail because we humans are good. In the workplace, taking the disastrous edge off arrogant or blind or lazy optimism is something worth striving for, because the effects of optimism can be profoundly damaging. A more balanced view of risks and rewards, opportunities and challenges, is crucial for creating a work environment where people can flourish and where the outputs of the business and of the people who work there can contribute to the healing of God's creation. But at a slightly deeper level, however empty or full we perceive the glass as being, the strength that we need to help us subvert that optimism, or to stand in its way, comes from knowing that there is no mark on the side of the glass up to which we should fill it, and beyond which we should not. The strength that we need comes from knowing that we cannot control everything, or even *anything*, comes from knowing that, nevertheless, we should still try to make things better because, whether we succeed or fail, God's grace, bought for us on the cross, will keep replenishing (and replacing) the glass however much we may mess up. That is mercy.

10

THE DEPRESSED COLLEAGUE

Hear my prayer, O Lord; let my cry come to
you. Do not hide your face from me in the day
of my distress. Incline your ear to me; answer
me speedily in the day when I call. For my days
pass away like smoke, and my bones burn like
a furnace. My heart is stricken and withered
like grass; I am too wasted to eat my bread.
Because of my loud groaning my bones cling to
my skin. I am like an owl of the wilderness, like
a little owl of the waste places. I lie awake; I am
like a lonely bird on the housetop. All day long
my enemies taunt me; those who deride me use
my name for a curse. For I eat ashes like bread,
and mingle tears with my drink, because of
your indignation and anger; for you have lifted
me up and thrown me aside. My days are like
an evening shadow; I wither away like grass.
Psalm 102:1–11 NRSV

It was February 1988. A beautiful winter's morning in London. Intense, low sunlight. I had just arrived at work, and was talking with the law partner I worked for. The phone rang. I was going to ignore it, but he waved me towards it: "No, no, go ahead, pick it up." It was a college friend, and she said three simple words: "Alexandra's killed herself."

Alexandra was bright, intelligent, charming, vivacious, funny – all the things that people say when a person dies young. But she really *was* all of those, and more. I'd last seen her a few weeks earlier, and we'd had a long chat that weekend morning before the others were up. She was quieter then, but that had seemed to me an inner stillness, a deep gentleness. A few days later her sister had told me she was feeling a little low, and could I write to her? I started a letter, intending to be upbeat, bright, amusing. But I couldn't quite find the words or the tone that I was looking for. So, I put it aside for a moment… and I have it still today, unfinished: a reminder of what might have been; a reminder of what was not to be.

Alexandra planned her death meticulously, and with huge concern for those close to her. It would happen while others were not around. The person she felt would be most able to cope with it would be the one who found her. But that care made it seem to us only more inexplicable. She had so much to give; so much to live for. But as time passed, it emerged that in the months before her death Alexandra had been clinically depressed. She hid it – largely – behind that bright, funny exterior. But she had been struggling; even been briefly hospitalized. And we, most of us, never knew, never even guessed. That was my first – but not, as it turned out, my last – encounter with clinical depression.

In most of what I've written in this book, I've been dealing with things that I know about and understand, and where practical solutions and processes may help – as may empathy; or really listening to someone; or just simple kindness. But there are some areas not so amenable to practical common sense, and mental illness is one of those. The writer of Psalm 102 captures some of this overwhelming sense of oppression, of desolation, of persecution, of abandonment, of lethargy, of sorrow, of being cast aside, of being left behind, of being totally forgotten. A mind in the grip of such intense, enduring, vivid sensations and thoughts truly is a different case.

Depression and illnesses of the mind[22]

I have used "depressed" in the title of this chapter, partly because depression is a recognized mental condition; partly because a depressed person may function in the workplace at a very high level while still being medically ill; and partly because I know it a little better than most others. But there are other mental health conditions, such as Obsessive Compulsive Disorder (OCD), Hoarding, and Attention Deficit Hyperactivity Disorder (just to name three of many possible others), which look different to depression but share a characteristic of depression, namely, that sufferers can still also function at a high level in the workplace. And the basic point I want to reinforce is that all of these conditions are mental

---

22 I am not going to cover the full range of mental conditions in this chapter, especially ones that may include frightening or even violent moments. So, I won't cover conditions that involve psychotic episodes; and nor will I cover conditions such as schizophrenia or bipolar disorder. It's not just because I know nothing about such conditions, but also because someone suffering, for example, psychotic episodes would not be in, or remain long in an office, or most other workplaces. Obviously, they should (and, most likely would, these days) be treated with great sympathy and compassion – but they would also be required to receive treatment and only return to work when the condition had been medically stabilized and did not, for example, represent a physical threat to fellow workers. The purpose of this chapter, therefore, is to look at a slightly narrower category of mental conditions, loosely grouped around depression, where our colleague, our neighbour in the office, may appear to be "fine" – but, in fact, really isn't.

illnesses, in the way that very different physical illnesses are still all "physical". So, what I write here when I refer primarily to "depression" can, I hope, with appropriate adaptation, be applied to these three and to many others.

While in the past thirty years we've come a long way in de-stigmatizing "mental illness", the term still carries baggage – we still hear those childhood taunts: "soft", "feeble", "mental", and worse – and however much we tell ourselves it's just the same as a physical illness, we don't, always, really believe it. Why? I'm not entirely sure, but even today it clearly has something to do with our perception of our mind (dating all the way back to Plato) being the essence of who we are in a way that our bodies aren't. Additionally, in some religious settings a mental condition is seen as the sign of a troubled soul, perhaps one tormented by sin, and, sometimes, also as some type of punishment. (I'll come back to that.) And even in the more secular parts of society, some stigma remains – perhaps because "mental illness" is associated with weakness; with not being able to "control" ourselves; with hysterics, panic, fear.

Another possible reason? Well, in relation to some conditions, maybe it is still seen by many as a pretext or a cover for lack of effort, lack of application, or even "sheer laziness". To look for a moment at a condition that emerges in childhood (although, later on, it does affect those in the workplace), when I was younger, I was dismissive of what seemed then to be an epidemic of ADHD diagnoses. It was, I arrogantly thought, a classic excuse: over-diagnosed, over-medicated, and over-whelmingly middle class. That was before I saw how my own child – who would previously have been labelled as lazy, clumsy, and inattentive – came academically alive when diagnosed and then treated. It's so easy to be casually dismissive of mental conditions until experience knocks us around a little.

One of the other things that I have really come to understand over time, clichéd though it sounds, is how very little I understand about mental illness. I am, for example, constantly caught off guard by how seemingly small events, even phrases, can throw some people totally off course. How what seems so rational, so obvious, so self-evidently beneficial to me (and, perhaps, to much of the rest of the world), may look to some others like an impassable crevice, an unclimbable mountain – or, perhaps, the very gates of hell.

But I've also seen how pharmaceutical drugs can sometimes work in remarkable ways where nothing else can, and this points back to the fundamental insight that our colleague is suffering from a medical condition, not a moral one. "Brain chemistry" sounds a rather abstract term, rather theoretical, until you come close to someone whose brain chemistry has changed. It is perhaps only then that you can appreciate that that chemical change also seemingly changes them, the "person". Suddenly for them, chemically, white has become black; day has become night; up has become down. And then it can be changed back again by medicine. It turns out that it's not laziness, or lack of determination, or lack of moral fibre that turned their world upside down. It's chemistry. Atoms and molecules.

Until the day I die I will never regard the brain as anything other than one of the most amazing, remarkable gifts we receive from God. But the idea that, because it is a gift, it defies all other physical rules and operates differently from – somehow apart from – the rest of our body, strikes me as absurd. So often we conceive of our brain, our mind, as something separate, the place where our personality, our soul, resides; as something distinct from the physical body which surrounds it. But that's just wrong: our personality, just as much as the movement of our limbs, as our heartbeat, as our breathing, is controlled by the brain, by reactions within it, by its physical and chemical composition. To be sure, I believe we (generally) have some control over whether to be good or bad; generous or selfish; kind or cruel. But what we do not have control over is whether to be depressed or not – any more than we do over developing cancer.

Body, mind, and spirit

How can we shake ourselves out of this way of thinking; put ourselves in a place where we can view mental conditions the same way as physical ones? Strangely, perhaps, I have found most useful not any medical book, but, rather, a short phrase from the old Book of Common Prayer which talks about us being troubled in "body, mind, or spirit". This makes, to me, a crucial distinction between our soul and our mind. We can be sick (troubled) in any of them. But to be troubled in our mind is not the same as being troubled in our soul – any more than being physically troubled equates to spiritual trouble. It puts treating the mind where it should be – on a par with treating the body. That's not to say that body, mind, and soul are not holistically linked in a way that some modern medicine does not always fully appreciate, and that, quite often, we will need to treat the soul in order to be able to treat effectively the body or the mind. But what that phrase does do is to place healing of the mind in the same context as healing of the body. I'll return to this in a moment when we look at "mercy".

Effects on the workplace

So, to move on to our central topic, how can a condition like depression affect the office? Well, potentially in a number of ways. To name three: in the effects on the depressed colleague;

in the effects on other individuals; and in the effects on the team and the business.

The effect on our depressed colleague

The effects on our depressed colleague can vary, but many of those variants come down to one word: "hiding". In some cases, because of the (perceived) stigma of depression – of mental illness more broadly – the colleague will seek to hide the problem. It's hard to hide a broken leg; but depression, OCD, and anxiety, for example, can all be effectively covered up ("No, no, I'm fine, just a momentary blip…"). Perhaps the colleague needs the regular salary; perhaps the job is the only thing that keeps them going, keeps their head above water, keeps the darkness just about at arm's length. But they fear that to show "weakness", to be thought incapable of doing the job, of withstanding the pressure, will lead to them losing their job. That may not be logical. Society has moved on considerably in its understanding over the last thirty years; and effective treatment for many conditions is available. But one of the most difficult things for people without such illnesses to understand is that those who do have them are often not amenable to this type of "rational" discussion. Because the brain is working differently, what to me seems sensible, clear, and obvious will not seem so to the depressed person. As the psalm writer says: "My days are like an evening shadow; I wither away like grass."

I'm a priest and a lawyer, not a doctor, so I won't venture further into medical territory – but an analogy which helps me to understand this a little is to recall how I sometimes feel when I wake in the middle of the night and start thinking (panicking, perhaps) about what seems to be a huge problem. I work out all sorts of fantastical, doom-laden scenarios, and, eventually, I fall back asleep convinced that nothing can go right. And then I get up in the morning, and, fully awake, in the daylight, with a renewed sense of perspective, I almost laugh at my night terrors. But they seemed completely rational, flawlessly logical, and very real back then. Looking at it like that, I think, may help us understand some of these conditions a little more.

There's another type of concealment which is slightly different, and goes, in part, to Alexandra's story at the beginning. This is not fear of losing the job, or of being thought weak. It's more the illness not wanting to be seen – hiding if you will, behind a screen of "normalcy" so that no one else ever knows.[23] We all do this to some extent. We have certain traits, characteristics, or, perhaps, things in our past that we simply don't want other people to see. And so, we hide them; or slightly change our own narrative to cover them up. But this is of a different magnitude and scale. Here almost everything is being hidden; one life is being lived behind another. Totally concealed. Not in every case will the outcome be the same as Alexandra's. But the strain of leading two, perhaps increasingly divergent lives – one that we can't talk about, and the other which seems a lie – can be enormous, overwhelming, and ultimately unbearable.

The effects on other individuals

I mentioned there can be an effect on other individuals in the workplace, and this, I think, is different from the effect on the team and on the work being done in that workplace. It goes to a sense of powerlessness, almost failure. Here you, as a neighbour,

---

23 A psychiatrist once told me that we should not call a person a "depressive", or an "anorexic", any more than we should call them a "cancer". Depression is a condition that a person has, which, to be sure, affects their daily life and human interactions, as does any physical illness. But it, nevertheless, remains a condition – a part of who they are, but not the only thing they are. The person – however much the illness may affect them – does not become the illness, and only the illness. Therefore, it is not an inherent part of a person's character that makes them hide the illness; it is a feature of the illness itself.

sense something is wrong with your colleague; you feel it, even if you can't quite put your finger on it. But unlike other issues such as family trouble, or money worries, you can't talk the person through it. Perhaps slightly helplessly, you just watch them. Perhaps you ask if they need help, but get politely rebuffed. Or, worst of all, you have what seems like a serious conversation, you think you've got somewhere, persuaded them of something to do, or something to change. And then it becomes clear that you've done nothing of the sort, that nothing at all has changed. Your words, your explanations, your suggestions – all totally ignored. You feel rejected and useless. But that's what mental illness can be like. It simply isn't "rational".

A slightly different effect that may impact the other individual comes from another aspect of "hiding". Perhaps the depressed colleague asks the second colleague to help them hide the condition from others. That second colleague then becomes part of the secret, part of the thing which is there, which other people in the workplace sense, but which is not being talked about. And that act of hiding then becomes a burden on two people, rather than on one.

The effects on the team and the workplace

Finally, there's the effect on the team, the workplace, and the business. Some of these effects are obvious, some slightly more subtle. At the obvious end: if someone really can't cope, if stress makes them sick, if they can't carry the full load of work, then other colleagues will have to pick up that work. There may well be sympathy for the depressed colleague, but that might not last for ever. There's also the effect on the work itself if it is not done well that we have also explored in other contexts. And, lastly – which is entirely possible given what we have looked at already – if the colleague seeks to hide the effect their illness has on their work, then any errors that they may have made might not emerge until it's too late to rectify them, with a further, and even more serious impact on the business as a whole.

Slightly different are the effects on the team and the atmosphere in the workplace if someone is severely depressed, or has another condition which is not (fully) disclosed and, yet, is in some way apparent. There's a feeling of imbalance, perhaps even unhappiness, which changes the dynamic and the atmosphere in the workplace. Or, perhaps, the boss, who is a manager not a therapist or psychiatrist, has to spend significant time with the depressed colleague helping them to do their job. The result of this is to divert attention away from other colleagues (or processes) who could benefit from, or who need that time. Time that would make those other colleagues more effective, more valuable, perhaps more fulfilled; or which would make the company more of a community, or add to the value that it brings to the world and to God's creation. But, instead, the manager is spending time on something they were not trained to do, don't feel good at, and which, at some point, may also begin to adversely, individually affect them.

Accepting mercy and showing mercy: a reversal

In all of the other chapters I have first discussed showing mercy, and, after that, discussed accepting it. However, in this chapter, because of the long history of looking down on mental conditions and the implication that those who suffered from them were, in some way, lesser human beings than us "normal" people, I have decided to reverse the order. In addition to that, it is also important for us to realize that "mental illness" is not binary. Many of these issues lie on a spectrum rather than being conditions that we either "have" or "don't have". Many of us have traits or conditions we ignore, the treatment of which – if we could only acknowledge and seek that treatment without ourselves feeling weak – could substantially improve our lives. And following on from that point, if we never acknowledge that we need mercy, then we will never accept healing; and if we never accept healing, then we will miss out on much of God's gift to us. So, while showing mercy to our depressed colleague is important, accepting our own need, and acknowledging our own weaknesses, are equally so.

Being the injured man: accepting mercy

Opening ourselves to our own need for mercy

So, what happens if we are the injured man lying in the road? As we've discussed before, rarely, in the narrative of our own lives, are we the weak one, the one in need of mercy, rather than the generous dispenser of it. And this issue is heightened in the case of depression and other mental conditions because – wherever we are on the spectrum of that illness – the illness itself may "persuade" us that we are not ill. Thus, the very practical side of my accepting mercy is some level of awareness that I may not know that I actually need that mercy – and, thus, that I need to accept the necessity of putting myself in the position where that need can be recognized by others. To give a rather prosaic example, every year I have a physical medical exam. While part of the reason is (relatively) latent hypochondria, part of the reason is to get a professional's read on whether there are aspects of my physical and mental health that need attention. To be sure, many of the tests are physical, but I am also asked about anxiety and stress, and some of the physical tests perform a dual role. And another example: I regard spiritual direction – although neither a psychiatric exam nor, primarily, a therapeutic exercise – as a form of mental (spiritual) health check.

Additionally, without unduly burdening family or friends, I do ask them to let me know if they think I am maintaining balance, not obsessing, not focusing too intently on one small (or even big) thing to the exclusion of all others. And, outside the circle of those we know, we can engage with a therapist – very definitely not a sign of weakness – who can investigate the roots of our anxieties and worries, and, where necessary, direct us towards more specialized psychiatric or psychological help. But the point in all of these examples is that accepting mercy is a two-step process which requires us, first, to put ourselves in the position where our need to have mercy shown to us can be ascertained (and that mercy offered); and, second, to then actually accept that mercy.

Beyond that, accepting mercy as the injured man for me, at least, means accepting the gift of the body/mind/spirit distinction. It means acknowledging that "perfection" of the physical and mental kind is not attainable in this world (short of the perfection of all things at the end of time). It also means, in addition to that acknowledgment, a further recognition that that "lack" of perfection – mental and/or physical – does not matter because our spirit, our soul, has already been forgiven, healed by the love of God. To be sure we can have physical and mental ailments that are incurable, and that, one day, will eventually kill us. But those can in many cases be controlled (if not "cured") and we can lead full lives. But truly accepting mercy is not just seeking medical help (important though that is), but, more fundamentally, acknowledging that you, I, can't do anything alone.

The healer needs healing

In the section below on "showing mercy", I discuss at some length the benefits of a church offering a healing service: a formal, structured (although, I hope, also sensitive and unpressured) process by which we can hand over our troubles to God. But in the category of "accepting mercy" – and in keeping with my concern that in situations of mental illness it is always the "sane" people who offer the mercy – I want to examine a particular aspect of that service. To be sure, the person (sometimes, but not always, a priest) who is laying on hands and anointing with oil, is the facilitator to help others share some of their extraordinarily heavy burdens with God. But, sometimes, it can feel more than that. It can feel like (to personalize it) I am actually bestowing the healing, rather than acting as an incredibly privileged facilitator and a conduit for God's grace. There are many dangers in that (arrogance, pride, etc.), but one very significant one can be that it enables me – as the strong healer – to hide from my own need for healing; to hide from my own need to understand and acknowledge what I cannot handle alone, and what needs God's healing.

So, as a structural element of the service, before I lay on hands and anoint others, I receive healing for myself. And, in that structure, I have to confront and acknowledge my own need for healing. In that space, in view of what I am about to try to facilitate for others, I never ask for a miraculous cure, or for any sort of perfection. But I do ask for healing of the mind. For healing of the things that trouble me in my mind; and for healing of those things that trouble members of my family in theirs. Things that doctors can help with, if not cure; and things where, in simply recognizing the issue, we can help each other. And in that sharing of my burden, that touch of someone else's hand on my shoulder, that cross made with oil by another person on my forehead, and that spoken reassurance of God's blessing given by another, I receive a sense of healing, of wholeness, of permission to deal with those issues – and of permission simply to live with them. That is mercy to me – but mercy I first must acknowledge that I need; that I must first open myself up to accept.

Being the Good Samaritan: showing mercy

So, having reversed the order and shown how I must first open myself to accepting mercy, what does showing mercy to our depressed colleague look like? To return to an earlier point, I think it's important to start off by saying that we, their colleagues, as non-medics, cannot provide mercy in the form of a diagnosis, much less a medical "cure". This is not like the shy, or verbose, or ambitious colleague. We, as non-medics, cannot reset the chemistry of someone's brain, or their compulsion, or their obsession, any more than we could ourselves reset their broken leg, prescribe them antibiotics, or stitch up their wounds. And it's really important that we realize this; otherwise our attempts at mercy will, at best, be ineffective, and, at worst, could be damaging. If we set out to cure something we do not understand, and for which we don't have the requisite skill, then real harm is a possibility.

How our business can show mercy

There are a number of practical things that a business can do, and that individuals can do. First, the business should make clear that (non-violent)[24] mental illness is no different from physical illness. It should be made crystal clear that both types of illness will give rise to the same health benefits, the same understanding, the same sympathy. If there is private insurance, both types of illness will be entitled to equal levels of treatment. Neither will disqualify you from a job that you are able to do, and both will entitle you to accommodations to allow you to continue to contribute as effectively as possible. If medical leave is required, then, equally, in either case, your job

---

24 As noted above, mental illnesses that involve the potential for violence, or other elements of highly emotional disruption, will have to be dealt with slightly differently – albeit still with compassion and with the same level of benefits available to other workers who have a physical illness.

will be preserved. All of this helps to regularize/normalize/ destigmatize mental conditions.

Second, in the same way that many businesses now encourage healthy physical lifestyle choices, including regular check-ups and assessments, they can do the same for mental health. Of course, there is always the concern that this becomes a little Orwellian – do you really want Big Brother knowing all this? But I think if you've got the first point (in the paragraph above) right, and people really believe that a mental condition will be treated identically to a physical illness, then the Big Brother-is-going-to-fire-me-for-being-weak concern diminishes. (And even if the mental condition is self-induced, then, as with physical conditions that are self-induced (e.g. by smoking), equally non-judgmental medical care should be available to help deal with the addiction or other issue that caused the mental condition.)

There is an obvious problem, however, with both of these, and that is the "hiding" or concealment issue. However generous the company seems to be, however genuinely the people appear to care, to a troubled mind that may nevertheless be processed as evidence of exactly the opposite. That may become evidence that they're seeking to weaken your defences, tempting you to come out from behind the wall, trying to lure you out into the open where you can be diminished and then destroyed. So, to deal with this unwillingness to take advantage of whatever help may be on offer – although this is obviously *very* delicate – colleagues should feel able to let their company know if they think that a fellow worker is depressed or affected by some other condition that could benefit from mental health-care.

But, as I said, it really is delicate. Few of us want to be seen as informing on a colleague; and others will worry that that is precisely the problem – that some people, for reasons of ambition, or from sheer unpleasantness, or even pure malice, would be very happy to have their colleagues thought of as "disabled" in any way. So perhaps you design a system which requires reporting to the business's medical team (or to an outside provider, or agency), where the information is kept confidential. Only in very specific circumstances, such as the possibility of self-harm, or serious harm to the business, will that information be shared with management or HR, absent the consent of the depressed colleague.

How we can show mercy: healing

All of these things that the business can do or enable to be done are valuable, and are an integral part of "showing mercy" broadly. But our involvement there is more in facilitating the eventual delivery of mercy by others, than in truly showing it ourselves. So how might we directly show mercy to our depressed colleague? To explore that, I'm going to return to and expand upon what I talked about in the previous section in relation to what happens during a religious healing service. The structure of the service is simple: after prayers and music, individuals come up to the altar rail. They say what type of healing they are looking for – for themselves or others, and for healing of the body, or mind, or soul, or some combination. The member of the healing team standing with them then prays aloud for that concern, while gently touching the person's shoulder or head. And finally, as the person is anointed with oil on their forehead they are told they should "Go in the healing love of God."

Healing as wholeness

As a priest – and this has been a real surprise to me – these are the most moving services in which I take part. When I was a layperson, I regarded this type of stuff with deep suspicion. This was precisely what hard-line televangelists got up to. Or it was hopelessly entangled in the superstitious, ritualistic mumbo-jumbo of the traditionalists. Either way it just wasn't for me.

But age and experience can, occasionally, be enlightening (not to mention humbling), and I have completely changed my view. It's something to do with looking – and this is a privilege unlike any other – into the face of another person, into the eyes of another person who realizes at that very moment that they are and always have been loved, that they are already forgiven, and that their future is more important than their past. It is only at that moment that I truly understand what healing is (and why it is, indisputably, a sacrament).

I keep using that word – healing – but what exactly do I mean by it? Well, and to be clear, I don't think healing = miraculous cure. It's not a magical return to "the way things were before". But what it does mean is a restoration of some type of "wholeness". Wholeness in relationships with others, and wholeness in our relationship with God. But also wholeness in the way we view our bodies and our lives. Wholeness is not about seeking perfection or total cure, but is a way of living with what we have in a way that enables us to have complete lives. Wholeness is dealing with what afflicts us not as a problem, or a defect, or even worse, some type of divine judgment, but as something which is a part of what we are, which needs to be acknowledged, but then needs to be placed in the context of a larger life – a life in which we are always loved by God.

On a more practical level, perhaps, healing is wholeness as in "wholeness" of treatment. If at that altar rail the person asks for healing related to a physical or mental concern, I am very careful to pray with that person not just for God's direct healing touch, but also for the skill of nurses and doctors, for the gifts of pharmaceutical drugs and psychiatric care. I try to make as clear as I can that these treatments administered by other human beings are as much a gift of – and from – God as any "miraculous" cure ever would be. Part of the mercy I can offer is my understanding (from my own experience) that God's healing can come through many channels and in many ways, all of them equally valid, none superior to the others, and all of which they should feel able to accept – to accept as a gift, freely given, without obligation.

And the one other aspect of mercy, linked to what I have just written about, is to emphasize the trinity of body, mind, and spirit. As I mentioned above, this is a powerful and liberating thought in itself, because it emphasizes the difference between mind and soul, as well as the similarity between body and mind. To be troubled in mind is not necessarily to be troubled in soul, and it is certainly no indication of the state of our relationship with God. And while troubles of the spirit may require spiritual healing, troubles of the mind are most definitely amenable to physical healing delivered by human beings, whether in the form of medication, psychiatric care, therapy, or any of the other increasingly broad array of treatments on offer.

Healing the spirit

But let me turn for a moment to healing of the spirit, where I can play a more direct role. The mercy that I can help deliver is reassurance to people that their sins are forgiven by God; that whatever afflicts them is not some divine punishment for a past failing; and that God truly loves them. I can tell them that while I understand (and have felt) the pain that the writer of Psalm 102 describes, I can also promise them that God does not hate them, and that God has completely forgiven them for everything they have ever done because He loves them, and He always has.

In other words, and put briefly: their soul is fine. That is the reassurance, the hope that Jesus gives to all those whom He cures throughout the Gospels: "Go, your sins have been forgiven," He always says. And with that reassurance, with that burden removed, those to whom we offer that mercy can go on to receive medical or therapeutic healing for the troubles of the mind, no longer concerned that their illness is a fault, a failing, a disease of their spirit. Instead they can see it for what it is – a problem, an issue, which perhaps cannot be "cured", but which can be alleviated and controlled, allowing them to live a life of wholeness.

Healing in the office

OK, you're thinking, but how does this work in the office? Oil and laying on of hands, for heaven's sake? Touching people and praying aloud? Well, to be sure, not physically. But I do believe that you can bring these healing acts – these healing gifts – metaphorically, into the workplace. For that to work, however, you need to do a few things. First, and most importantly, you need to listen very carefully to your colleague – both to what is being said and is not being said. Is there even a suggestion, a hint, a murmur that there is a mental health problem? If so, that will be beyond your capabilities to treat, but you can then gently make the point to them that to seek medical care is not weak or a sign of failure, but, in fact, actually what they need and what they should do. Also, are they confusing what troubles them in mind with something being wrong spiritually? If so, again very gently, you may be able to help disentangle that and reassure them that illness of the mind is not the same as illness of the soul. And, finally – and this is the closest we get to laying on of hands and anointing in the office setting – you can let them know, in the most secular terms that you feel you need to, that whatever their illness may be, their soul, their conscience, their character, is clean and in the clear. If we can do that, then we can give them the sacramental gift: the permission, if you will, to seek help for their mind and to forgive themselves, while not also thinking themselves weak. Put slightly differently, we can give them the gift of hope.

So, if we explain, if necessary in non-religious language, how we understand the body/mind/spirit division, we can demonstrate that seeking help is not a failing, or a weakness, or some type of trap, but is actually the way out of trouble. And in doing all of that, even in secular language, in a secular setting, with only metaphorical hands and metaphorical oil, we can still bring God's mercy into the workplace. We can bring the knowledge that help – from us, and from the medical profession – is always available, and comes free from judgment on our side, and free from anything that requires guilt on theirs. That is truly mercy.

But I want to finish this chapter where I began – with Alexandra. I still so wish that thirty years ago I had been able to write any of this to her. That I could have let her understand, let her feel, any of this sense of mercy. But I couldn't, because I didn't know enough; and perhaps because I hadn't yet lived enough. Maybe, at last, however, this completes that long-unfinished letter – started to her, but finished now to be read by others.

It is late, and still imperfect. But it comes now with far more understanding, even greater appreciation, and, as it always did, with much love.

AFTERWORD

REFLECTING IN THE MIDST OF THE STORM – THE DEPARTING COLLEAGUE

When I started writing this book eighteen months ago, my father was still alive, it seemed inconceivable that Britain could vote to leave the EU, and Donald Trump was not considered an even semi-serious candidate for the Republican nomination, far less the presidency of the United States. How the world changes...

One other thing also seemed settled. At that point I had been at GE just over fifteen years (five times longer than in any other job) and seemed set to complete the last six years of my career there. A reasonable glide path to sixty, and a comfortable pension looked within reach. However, as it turned out, nor was that to be. In the autumn/fall of 2016, GE decided that with the changing shape of the company, and pressure on costs, they had only two choices: drastically reduce the size of the tax department, or find a way of keeping the department intact somewhere else. They chose the latter route, and negotiated a deal with PricewaterhouseCoopers, one of the "Big 4" accounting firms, for them to take on almost the entire corporate tax department. It is an innovative, audacious, in many ways generous, and in many ways scary, plan.

As I write this, that plan is still two months away from execution (although by the time you read this it will already have been in operation for several months). But right in the middle of something – despite the possibility of getting the future completely wrong – there can be an immediacy to theological reflection that is lacking in a more measured analysis undertaken some time after the event. So, following the structure of the rest of this book, in miniature, I want to consider where I and my colleagues are right now, look at what mercy to them might look like, and then look at what mercy to me might be.

In the maelstrom

For almost everyone, this dropped from a clear blue sky. People knew that costs needed to be cut, and that jobs would be lost. But something of this scale was not expected. And more than that, it was inconceivable in advance of it occurring. It was like looking at a large building being demolished by explosives. One moment it was there, the next it wasn't. But you could not previously have conceived of it not being there. Crumbling; getting dirtier; windows being broken? Yes, all of those. But it simply not being there? Something of substance, which fully occupied a space and had done so for ever (or so it seemed), all of a sudden gone? Unimaginable.

So, the first reaction of many was not grief or anger, but bemusement and incomprehension – looking at the empty space where the seemingly solid building had been, not quite able to comprehend that it was, suddenly, no longer there. For some (I write this two weeks after the announcement), the numbness is wearing off and there are a range of emotions and concerns beginning to surface:

- Some are angry that what was often called the "best tax firm" (and certainly the "best tax department") in the world has suddenly been vaporized.

- Others are scared about what it means for their future. Are their jobs at PwC secure? Will they have enough work? Are they expected to hustle for business? What about work–life balance?

- Others had run (sometimes, almost literally, screaming) from the accounting and law firms to the haven of working inside a company. They had made a definite, positive choice to leave that environment, and now they will be going back. For them it seems (currently) like having their parole revoked and being sent back to jail.

- Others worry about what it means for benefits such as pensions, or healthcare, or other things which had, over the years, gone in their minds from highly speculative possibilities to baked-in probabilities.

- And, finally, others see the opportunities of the new arrangement, and value the possibility (although far from guaranteed) of keeping together a team that feels like a community, a neighbourhood, almost a family.

Showing mercy

Showing mercy: listening

Virtually all of the ways of showing mercy are those we have discussed before: not offering bromides and happy talk up-front, but listening (really hard) to people to discover where the hurt, where the concerns, where the problems really are. For example, why did they run away from the accounting firm ten years ago? Was it the work–life balance? Was it the nature of the work? Or was it, rather, an interaction with a particular person (a boss, a colleague) that deeply wounded them and which they cannot now disassociate from the place where that happened? Or why are they angry? Is it really because something beautiful has been suddenly obliterated, or is there something else going on? Are they perhaps scared that after several years in a certain environment they won't be able to fit into another one? Or, perhaps, they are scared that some of their skills have atrophied and they will be "found out"? As always, to be effective in showing mercy, we need to deal with causes not symptoms, so first we have to listen.

If we can discern the underlying causes, then we may be able to begin to address them. As appropriate, we can offer assurances that certain things will not change, and that they are not exchanging a rest farm for a sweatshop. We can also explain that other things will change – but give an explanation that demystifies those changes, taking (hopefully) much of the fear and apprehension out of them. And we can also point out the positives. It will keep the team together. More than that, it will also mean working in a place where the reputation of the GE tax department has inspired something approaching awe. There will be opportunities to do new things with new people at a firm where tax is the centre of their lives (rather than being seen – even at GE sometimes – as a service department rather than a core function).

Showing mercy: looking forwards, not backwards

But the greatest mercy may be to build on the simple, and irrefutable, point that what we had before could not have continued indefinitely into the future. Times (and GE) had dramatically changed, and the old structure was unsustainable. Something had to be done. That much is straightforward, but I also want to build in a theological point here. Nostalgia, harking back to a golden age, a desire to live in the past, is not a Christian attitude. There is a very famous poem by the British writer Matthew Arnold called "Dover Beach". After first talking of what he called the "eternal note of sadness" in the sound of the ebbing tide, he turns to the decline of Christianity:

> The Sea of Faith
> Was once, too, at the full, and round earth's shore
> Lay like the folds of a bright girdle furl'd.
> But now I only hear
> Its melancholy, long, withdrawing roar,
> Retreating, to the breath
> Of the night-wind, down the vast edges drear
> And naked shingles of the world.

There is something so seductively inviting about the falling cadences, particularly of that line: "Its melancholy, long, withdrawing roar". It invites us, too, to become melancholy; to look inwards; to look back with longing at a better time when all the world believed. For Matthew Arnold, that day was already gone – a memory of what had been, carried away by the night-wind – exposing the world in all its dreary ugliness. And it's that same emotion that is at work among some of my colleagues when, unhappy at the present and the future, they look longingly back to the way things were in the halcyon days at GE, and yearn intensely, and impossibly, to return to that time.

Well, you might say, it's not always particularly helpful to be trapped in the past, but what's unchristian about that? Well, here's what. While, of course, we can give thanks for past events and can remember with gratitude, the message of Christianity has *always* been that the best is yet to come. Jesus died on the cross precisely so we might have a better future, not a better past. Even if the present seems harder, more difficult, more unpleasant than a rose-tinted view of yesterday, it is, in fact, in the future when things will truly be better. Because it is then that everything shall be perfected, and every tear will be wiped away, and crying and pain will be no more (Revelation 21:4). Put simply, if the past is better than the future, then Christ died in vain. And that I do not believe. He died that we might look forward in hope, not backward in nostalgia.

So, to return to the current case, mercy to our colleagues is encouraging them to look for the opportunity in the change – and there will be opportunity. And mercy will be encouraging them to hope. To be sure we must be realistic – as well as empathetic to those who are worried or scared (or angry or grieving). There will certainly be the short-term pain of dislocation, and not everything will be as good as before. But we should also point out that something had to change, and that there is something inventive, something intentionally hopeful, in this arrangement.[25]

Showing mercy: the benefits of change

I wrote in *Where is God at Work?* about the unexpected benefits of receiving a P45/pink slip. I wrote that chapter distanced from the events by almost twenty years – but now, here I (sort of) am again (although with a very strong safety net beneath me). Yet, even in the midst of this one, I feel much the same way about both events. While it would have been extremely comfortable to stay, there is something new and fresh in the challenge. Something which can make us more alive. My job at GE was interesting, the people great, the atmosphere nourishing. But I could also see it looking much the same until I retired. I'd got most of the rhythms sorted out, and most of

---

25 Of course, and to state the very obvious, for this to mean anything, the two employers (old and new) must make the leaving simple and fair, and the arrival welcoming and rewarding.

the challenges fairly well in hand. Now I face new colleagues, new networks, new ways of working, new types of work, new challenges to overcome, new people to persuade. And the prospect is enticing, exciting. It goes back, in a way, to the parable of the talents. Are we content to bury our one talent in the ground and preserve it? Or do we take it, and, throwing caution to the winds, risk everything to grow it, risk everything in order to be more alive?

So, the mercy I would offer to others is the knowledge, the assurance (gained the hard way) that change – even though it looks like the end of something wonderful, and feels painful, even wrenching – can be the start of something more exciting, something with more life in it, the possibility to be creative again, to think in new ways. That sounds totally glib, of course, but it is truly heartfelt. There is something so life-enhancing if you can open yourself to the opportunity (and, for Christians, to the Holy Spirit), and wherever it is that it may be taking you.

Accepting mercy

So, the mercy that I can offer as the potential Good Samaritan to my neighbours at work is to listen and offer support; to encourage others to look forward not backward; and, finally, to point out the benefits of change. But while the first of those is pastorally sound, and all three are, I think, theologically sound, they are also just a little Pollyannaish. Well, that's me. So, the moment I heard about this transaction, I started planning. How did I make sure my team was all right? Whom in the new organization should I reach out to? What types of new things could I do? And, yes, how could I ensure I got the right benefits and rewards? I didn't pause to regret – I just determinedly, and at once, started to move forward.

But, some might say, to jettison what is now almost seventeen years of history with barely a murmur of regret or a backward glance seems somewhat callous or, at the very least, slightly emotionally disconnected. So perhaps mercy to me is to get me to pause, to look back at least a little, and to grieve with others for at least a while.

To a certain extent, particularly as we grow older, we have to harden our hearts. In the last half-year, I have buried my father, and helped move my mother out of the (beautiful, much-loved) family home of thirty years. So, I shut down just a bit in order to cope with that. And now this, too. I could argue I'm just currently out of emotional energy – but it probably goes deeper than that. English boarding schools have kept generations of therapists busy, and while my issue from those days is relatively minor, here's what it may be. From the age of ten, I left home to go to schools which, for at least the early years, I did not much enjoy (it got better after that). Leave, come back; leave, come back; leave. In the earliest years, I was terribly homesick and emotionally overwhelmed at the start of each term; but, slowly, I hardened up. To leave – to avoid that reflex of being hurt again and again – I just shut down, and didn't look back. University was a little different as it was such a positive experience. But, with jobs, however much I've enjoyed doing them – and with houses, however much I've enjoyed living in them – when I leave, I leave. No looking back. That's the way it's been for over forty years.

But, actually, to mourn a little, to remember with gratitude, love even, what has been lost, is profoundly human. And not to mourn, to stride out of the door without a backwards glance, is a way of avoiding grief, to be sure, but one that suppresses that grief and locks it away – rather than looking at it, staying with it a while, coming to terms with it, and then, at last, gently putting it aside before walking on. Mercy, to me, is pointing this out and inviting me to linger a while to consider the pain, the grief, of my neighbours, as well as remembering the pleasures and the joys of the last seventeen years. There really is much to look forward to, but there is also much to be thankful for. Not dwelling on the past, not seeking to return there, not hiding from the future – no nostalgia – but, rather, remembering with gratitude what we had, giving thanks, and then moving on. To have been reminded of that is mercy indeed.

So, these are my reflections in the midst of the storm. Reflections more raw than they will be with the benefit of hindsight, but perhaps also slightly more honest for being so immediate. Yet to tie this back to the rest of the book in a final thought, these reflections are guided by the knowledge that, whatever happens, the Good Samaritan – Jesus – is always coming down the road towards us, always ready to bind our wounds, and always ready to carry us off to safety and care for us. Because of that, however dark the present may seem, we know that we are always loved, and that we will never be abandoned. And because of that, we also know, truly, that the future is always brighter.